The Teaching and Learning of Social Research Methods

The importance of the teaching and learning of social research methods is increasingly recognised by research councils and policy bodies as crucial to the drive to increase capacity amongst the research community. The need for greater scholarly engagement with how research methods are taught and learnt is also driven by the realisation that epistemological and methodological developments have not been accompanied by a pedagogical literature or culture. Training initiatives need this pedagogic input if they are to realise the educational aspirations for methodologically skilled and competent researchers, able to apply, adapt and reflect on a range of high-level research methods and approaches. The contributors to this collection have fully engaged with this need to develop and share pedagogical knowledge in relation to the teaching of research methods. Together they span qualitative, quantitative and mixed methods, a range of disciplinary and national contexts, and face-to-face and blended teaching and learning. Through detailed examples, the collection addresses how best teaching practices develop in response to distinctive challenges that will resonate with readers; in so doing it will inspire and inform their own development.

This book was originally published as a special issue of the *International Journal of Social Research Methodology*.

Melanie Nind is professor of education at the University of Southampton, UK, where she is a co-director of the ESRC National Centre for Research Methods (NCRM) and principal investigator for the 'Pedagogy of Methodological Learning' study.

Daniel Kilburn is a teaching fellow at University College London, UK, and was the research fellow on the NCRM study, 'Capacity building in social science research methods: Researching teaching and learning processes' (2013–2014).

Rebekah Luff is senior research fellow at NCRM.

The Teaching and Learning of Social Research Methods

Developments in pedagogical knowledge

Edited by
Melanie Nind, Daniel Kilburn and Rebekah Luff

LONDON AND NEW YORK

First published 2017
by Routledge
2 Park Square, Milton Park, Abingdon, Oxon, OX14 4RN, UK

and by Routledge
711 Third Avenue, New York, NY 10017, USA

Routledge is an imprint of the Taylor & Francis Group, an informa business

Chapters 1–5 © 2017 Taylor & Francis
Chapter 6 © Louise Corti and Veerle Van den Eynden
Chapter 7 © Melanie Nind, Daniel Kilburn and Rose Wiles

All rights reserved. No part of this book may be reprinted or reproduced or utilised in any form or by any electronic, mechanical, or other means, now known or hereafter invented, including photocopying and recording, or in any information storage or retrieval system, without permission in writing from the publishers.

Trademark notice: Product or corporate names may be trademarks or registered trademarks, and are used only for identification and explanation without intent to infringe.

British Library Cataloguing in Publication Data
A catalogue record for this book is available from the British Library

ISBN 13: 978-1-138-20035-7

Typeset in Times New Roman
by RefineCatch Limited, Bungay, Suffolk

Publisher's Note
The publisher accepts responsibility for any inconsistencies that may have arisen during the conversion of this book from journal articles to book chapters, namely the possible inclusion of journal terminology.

Disclaimer
Every effort has been made to contact copyright holders for their permission to reprint material in this book. The publishers would be grateful to hear from any copyright holder who is not here acknowledged and will undertake to rectify any errors or omissions in future editions of this book.

Contents

Citation Information   vii
Notes on Contributors   ix

Introduction: The teaching and learning of social research methods: developments in pedagogical knowledge   1
Melanie Nind, Daniel Kilburn and Rebekah Luff

1. The problems and prospects in the teaching of mixed methods research   9
   Sharlene Hesse-Biber

2. 'I'm not a quants person'; key strategies in building competence and confidence in staff who teach quantitative research methods'   25
   Julie Scott Jones and John E. Goldring

3. Embedding quantitative skills into the social science curriculum: case studies from Manchester   41
   Jennifer Buckley, Mark Brown, Stephanie Thomson, Wendy Olsen and Jackie Carter

4. Teaching social research methods after the critical turn: challenges and benefits of a constructivist pedagogy   57
   Cosmo Howard and Michelle Brady

5. From guided-instruction to facilitation of learning: the development of *Five-level QDA* as a CAQDAS pedagogy that explicates the practices of expert users   73
   Christina Silver and Nicholas H. Woolf

6. Learning to manage and share data: jump-starting the research methods curriculum   91
   Louise Corti and Veerle Van den Eynden

7. Using video and dialogue to generate pedagogic knowledge: teachers, learners and researchers reflecting together on the pedagogy of social research methods   107
   Melanie Nind, Daniel Kilburn and Rose Wiles

Index   123

Citation Information

The chapters in this book were originally published in the *International Journal of Social Research Methodology*, volume 18, issue 5 (September 2015). When citing this material, please use the original page numbering for each article, as follows:

Editorial
The teaching and learning of social research methods: developments in pedagogical knowledge
Melanie Nind, Daniel Kilburn and Rebekah Luff
International Journal of Social Research Methodology, volume 18, issue 5 (September 2015), pp. 455–461

Chapter 1
The problems and prospects in the teaching of mixed methods research
Sharlene Hesse-Biber
International Journal of Social Research Methodology, volume 18, issue 5 (September 2015), pp. 463–477

Chapter 2
'I'm not a quants person'; key strategies in building competence and confidence in staff who teach quantitative research methods'
Julie Scott Jones and John E. Goldring
International Journal of Social Research Methodology, volume 18, issue 5 (September 2015), pp. 479–494

Chapter 3
Embedding quantitative skills into the social science curriculum: case studies from Manchester
Jennifer Buckley, Mark Brown, Stephanie Thomson, Wendy Olsen and Jackie Carter
International Journal of Social Research Methodology, volume 18, issue 5 (September 2015), pp. 495–510

Chapter 4
Teaching social research methods after the critical turn: challenges and benefits of a constructivist pedagogy
Cosmo Howard and Michelle Brady
International Journal of Social Research Methodology, volume 18, issue 5 (September 2015), pp. 511–525

CITATION INFORMATION

Chapter 5
From guided-instruction to facilitation of learning: the development of Five-level QDA *as a CAQDAS pedagogy that explicates the practices of expert users*
Christina Silver and Nicholas H. Woolf
International Journal of Social Research Methodology, volume 18, issue 5 (September 2015), pp. 527–543

Chapter 6
Learning to manage and share data: jump-starting the research methods curriculum
Louise Corti and Veerle Van den Eynden
International Journal of Social Research Methodology, volume 18, issue 5 (September 2015), pp. 545–559

Chapter 7
Using video and dialogue to generate pedagogic knowledge: teachers, learners and researchers reflecting together on the pedagogy of social research methods
Melanie Nind, Daniel Kilburn and Rose Wiles
International Journal of Social Research Methodology, volume 18, issue 5 (September 2015), pp. 561–576

For any permission-related enquiries please visit:
http://www.tandfonline.com/page/help/permissions

Notes on Contributors

Michelle Brady, PhD, is a lecturer in sociology in the School of Social Science at the University of Queensland. Her research interests are in the areas of interpretive policy studies and critical family studies.

Mark Brown is a senior lecturer in the School of Social Sciences at the University of Manchester. He has wide experience of teaching quantitative methods at undergraduate and postgraduate level, and held a number of research grants in the field of curriculum innovation. He is currently co-director of the Manchester University Q-Step Centre.

Jennifer Buckley is a research associate in the Cathie Marsh Institute for Social Research, University of Manchester. She has experience of providing data support services as part of the UK Data Service and uses large scale comparative survey data in her research on public attitudes and behaviour.

Jackie Carter is director for Engagement with Research Methods Training in the Cathie Marsh Institute for Social Research, University of Manchester. She is co-director of the Manchester Q-Step Centre where she leads on placing undergraduate students into data-driven, real world summer internships. Jackie was formerly a secondary school mathematics teacher and latterly the director of Jorum, the UK National repository for open educational resources.

Louise Corti is an associate director of the UK Data Archive and head of the Collections Development and Producer Support teams. She has directed ESRC research data policy and sharing activities since 1995, she also leads on qualitative data activities at the Archive.

John E. Goldring is the deputy director of the Q-Step Centre and a senior lecturer in the Department of Sociology at Manchester Metropolitan University. He was the co-investigator of the ESRC RDI project, 'No More Point Clicky, numbers stuff; building staff quantitative skills' (2011–2014).

Sharlene Hesse-Biber is professor of sociology and director of the Women and Gender Studies Program at Boston College in Chestnut Hill, Massachusetts. She is currently leading a study exploring the lived experiences of both men and women with breast cancer.

Cosmo Howard, PhD, is a senior lecturer in the School of Government and International Relations and member of the Centre for Governance and Public Policy at Griffith University, Australia, specialising in comparative public management, autonomous state agencies and theories of individualisation.

NOTES ON CONTRIBUTORS

Julie Scott Jones is the director of the Q-Step Centre and associate head of the Department of Sociology at Manchester Metropolitan University. She was the principal investigator on the ESRC RDI project, 'No More Point Clicky, numbers stuff; building staff quantitative skills' (2011–2014).

Daniel Kilburn is a teaching fellow at University College London and was the research fellow on the ESRC National Centre for Research Methods study, 'Capacity building in social science research methods: Researching teaching and learning processes' (2013–2014).

Rebekah Luff is senior research fellow at NCRM.

Melanie Nind is professor of education at the University of Southampton where she is a co-director of the ESRC National Centre for Research Methods and principal investigator for the 'Pedagogy of Methodological Learning' study. She is co-editor of the *International Journal of Research & Method in Education*.

Wendy Olsen has 25 years' experience of teaching research methods, usually in interdisciplinary contexts. She has produced two textbooks on research methods. She is interested in realism, comparative case-study approaches, discourse analysis and the use of qualitative coding software for mixed methods.

Christina Silver, PhD, is the manager of the CAQDAS Networking Project (CNP) and co-director of the Day Courses in Social Research programme, both at the University of Surrey. Her research interests include the pedagogy of advanced methods teaching, uses and applications of CAQDAS technology, qualitative and mixed methods analysis, and the relationship between technology and methodology. She had a lead role in research conducted under the National Centre for Research Methods (NCRM) funded project Qualitative Innovations in CAQDAS (QUIC).

Stephanie Thomson is a research associate at the Manchester Institute of Education (MIE), University of Manchester. She is interested in critical mathematics education and comparative case-study approaches to data analysis.

Veerle Van den Eynden manages the Research Data Management team at the UK Data Archive. She leads on a variety of research and development projects on research data management and actively supports ESRC data policy activities.

Rose Wiles was a co-director of the ESRC National Centre for Research Methods and co-investigator on the ESRC National Centre for Research Methods study, 'Capacity building in social science research methods: Researching teaching and learning processes' (2013–2014).

Nicholas H. Woolf, PhD, is an independent qualitative research educator and a consultant in Santa Barbara, California, and most recently a visiting academic fellow at the University of Reading. As a qualitative research consultant, he has conducted research and published in numerous fields including public health, management, education and performance evaluation. His own research interests include the pedagogy of advanced qualitative methods teaching and the cognitive aspects of qualitative data analysis, and he is a co-author of an upcoming textbook, *Five-level QDA: A method for learning to use QDA software powerfully*.

INTRODUCTION

The teaching and learning of social research methods: developments in pedagogical knowledge

Introduction

Social research methods have been taught in a systematic and widespread way within Western academia for much of the past century. With increasing demands facing the social research community – whether from funders, universities, or the public – building and sustaining the methodological capacity to navigate challenging and unfamiliar empirical terrain is becoming ever more important. Yet despite this, to date the teaching and learning of research methods has occupied a comparatively marginal position within broader methodological discussions in the social sciences. In this special issue on developments of pedagogical knowledge in social research methods, established researchers from a range of social science disciplines, international contexts, and methodological orientations engage with questions of how research methods are taught and learnt.

Research capacity and methods training

In recent years, interest surrounding the advancement of research capacity and the role of methods training in enhancing that capacity has grown. This is a concern shared by universities, employers, and those involved in the governance and funding of higher education and social research at a national level in the case of the UK (BIS, 2014) and at a supranational level in the case of the EU (Kottmann, 2011). Arguments have emerged around the importance of advancing training in research methods to build capacity within the workforce to undertake sophisticated research tasks in response to current social challenges. A discursive and institutional connection between research capacity, individual employability and collective competitiveness therefore appears increasingly pervasive.

The provision of teaching and instruction in social research methods has been established since the turn of the twentieth century, with the publication of instructional manuals for researchers from the 1900s (Peden & Carroll, 2009) and the growth of social science degree courses in post-War Western Europe (Bulmer, 1985). Today, some form of structured research methods training is incorporated into undergraduate and graduate education in the majority of social sciences programmes. In the past, most social science graduates might have expected a career in social research (Bulmer, 1985), but today's graduates are less likely to follow such career paths. Methods training increasingly constitutes a source of transferable skills thought to enhance employability in a wider range of sectors. Simultaneously, those seeking to pursue a career in social science are expected to demonstrate methodological capability through 'advanced' training (additional to gaining experience from doctoral or post-doctoral research). Overall, this has meant an expansion in the provision of research methods teaching and training in structured degree and standalone short courses.

Developing and sustaining research capacity are integral to policy concerns regarding global competitiveness within national and disciplinary research communities. For example, the UK government posits research capacity as 'a critical asset for the UK, providing a competitive advantage in the global race for prosperity' (BIS, 2014, p. 5). This has fostered renewed interest in research methods training, particularly large-scale investments in quantitative methods. The Q-Step programme was launched in 2014 as a £19.5 million partnership between Nuffield Foundation, ESRC and HEFCE, to build undergraduate quantitative skills as a pipeline for capacity development. The ESRC's National Centre for Research Methods (NCRM) is now in its third term of funding to develop the quality and range of methodological approaches amongst UK social scientists. Other investments include the ESRC's Advanced Training Initiative and Scotland's Applied Quantitative Methods Network.

Investments are working to change the formal training landscape. Yet, despite the powerful discourse, increased funding, and structural changes to training provision, comparatively little attention has been paid to the question of *how* research methods are taught and learnt. This tension has led, in part, to this special issue of *International Journal of Social Research Methodology*.

Developments in pedagogic knowledge for research methods

Despite the attention given to research methods, there has been surprisingly little academic engagement with the pedagogical dimension. Pedagogy is concerned not just with what people do in teaching and learning situations but with what they perceive to be meaningful, important and relevant. While initiatives might recognise the importance of the quality of teaching and learning, there remain few sources of detailed or systematic insights into research methods pedagogy. Researchers of pedagogy in other domains have established the need to explore pedagogy as specified, enacted, and experienced (Nind, Curtin, & Hall, in press). For the most part, these aspects of pedagogy have been under-explored in debates over research capacity building.

(Wagner, Garner, & Kawulich, 2011) argue that a 'pedagogical culture' surrounding social research methods is lacking. Their systematic review of the literature identified neither 'a substantial research base' nor 'systematic discussions' on most aspects of teaching research methods (Wagner et al., 2011, p. 75). Later reviews have echoed these findings with (Earley, 2014) suggesting that comparatively little attention has been paid to questions of *how* certain research methods are taught within higher education. With few insights to inform their practice those who teach research methods, he argues, must instead 'rely on a network of peers, scattered research literature, and much trial-and-error' (Earley, 2014, p. 243). From a methods learner perspective, there have been few opportunities to engage in pedagogical research.

While there remains a dearth of pedagogical discourse concerning capacity building (Nind, Kilburn, & Wiles, 2014), there have been indicators of developing pedagogical knowledge surrounding the teaching of research methods. There are edited collections on teaching methods (Garner, Wagner, & Kawulich, 2009), some focused on quantitative (Payne & Williams, 2011) and qualitative methods (Hurworth, 2008) and others which are discipline specific (e.g. Adriaensen, Kerremans, & Slootmaeckers, 2015;

Loxley, Seery, & Grenfell, 2013). The UK Higher Education Academy (HEA) has funded a series of projects culminating in online resources and events (see HEA, 2015). NCRM has also consulted on the training needs amongst the UK methods community (Moley, Wiles, & Sturgis, 2013) and supported a growing strand of pedagogical research into advanced-level teaching and learning of research methods (Kilburn, Nind, & Wiles, 2014b) – on which one of the papers in the special issue is based (Nind et al., 2014). Explorations of novel uses of data to teach research methods (Bishop, 2012) and of the learning processes involved in working as a research group (Hernández-Hernández & Sancho-Gil, in press) have also featured in this journal. This expansion in the depth and breadth of engagement represents 'cause for optimism regarding the state of pedagogical practice and enquiry' (Kilburn, Nind, & Wiles, 2014a, p. 204). Indeed, current research within NCRM is seeking better understanding of pedagogic practices in social research methods and working to foster stronger pedagogic culture (http://pedagogy.ncrm.ac.uk).

One possible explanation for the lack of pedagogical research pertaining to research methods is that the disciplinary and methodological interests of those engaged in teaching research methods outstrip their pedagogical interest and expertise. In a competitive rather than altruistic academic culture, they may perceive little gain in researching and publishing on their pedagogic practice. Pedagogy is about ideas, values and traditions as well as practices; while it is an elusive concept, grasping it allows for stronger engagement with what matters in the competent application of research methods. This special issue constitutes a considerable step towards addressing the gaps in research generating pedagogical knowledge. The authors of the papers have taken up various, and often urgent calls to reflect upon pedagogical matters. We acknowledge the role of the reviewers[1] in providing feedback in this process.

The special issue considers a range of methods learners including undergraduates from Canada (Howard & Brady, 2015) and the UK (Buckley, Brown, Thomson, Olsen, & Carter, 2015; Scott Jones & Goldring, 2015), post-graduates from USA (Hesse-Biber, 2015), and researchers on short-courses (Corti & Van den Eynden, 2015; Nind, Kilburn, & Wiles, 2015; Silver & Woolf, 2015). Most of the papers are reflective case studies of pedagogical practice development, with two examples funded by the ESRC's quantitative methods teaching initiatives (Buckley et al., 2015; Scott Jones & Goldring, 2015). One paper (Nind et al., 2015) goes beyond the authors' own practice to address methods of researching pedagogy with teachers and learners. While the methods being taught vary across the papers, similar challenges and pedagogical themes emerge: teachers as learners; the lack of pedagogical culture to support methods teaching and learning; the role of reflection; the varied background, attitudes and approaches of learners; and the role of methods software in teaching and learning.

Hesse-Biber (2015) highlights difficulties relating to the teaching and learning of mixed methods, with a key challenge being the lack of methods expertise of teaching staff. This is echoed in the quantitative teaching papers of Buckley et al. (2015) and Scott Jones and Goldring (2015) addressing how teaching staff can lack confidence in their methods skills and their ability to teach it. Both Hesse-Biber (2015) and Buckley et al. (2015) demonstrate that the introduction of, or structural changes to, teaching teams can enhance teacher expertise. Corti and Van den Eynden (2015) describe the pressure on those teaching data management to be familiar with new data resources and agendas, largely developing teaching resources 'from scratch'.

Similarly, Silver and Woolf (2015) elucidate how pedagogy can facilitate learners' ability to harness the increasing power and complexity of Computer Assisted Qualitative Analysis (CAQDAS) software. Scott Jones and Goldring (2015) focus on the issue of 'training the trainers', setting out a framework for staff to learn quantitative methods at same time as learning how to teach them. The deficiency of pedagogical culture to support methods teaching and learning is apparent throughout the special issue. Scott Jones and Goldring's case study of successfully upskilling methods teachers emphasises that teachers, as well as learners, require incentives, time, support and resources. The study further demonstrates the benefits of reflecting on learning and practice, both for teachers and students alike.

Reflection is both a key pedagogic theme but also the dominant research method within the set of papers, with the majority involving methods teachers reflecting systematically on teaching and learning. Nind et al. (2015) combine the reflection of trainers with that of learners through focus group dialogue supported by video playback of that day's teaching experience. This generates research data and provides teachers with the opportunity to consider their teaching experience in a way that can inform their practice. Silver and Woolf (2015) also reflect on how new pedagogies were developed in response to challenges to teaching and learning that became apparent only as CAQDAS training evolved. The focus on the teaching of advanced methods in short-course format highlights the considerable challenge in knowing how to teach a method in the face of diverse and sometimes ill-prepared learners. This challenge is echoed by Hesse-Biber (2015), with mixed methods learners perhaps being weaker in qualitative or quantitative methods respectively and finding mixed methods to be a departure from their methodological preconceptions. Once again, encouraging reflexivity, this time in learners, is argued to be key to progressing learning. Similarly, Howard and Brady (2015) propose that using self-reflection within a constructivist pedagogy can turn the scepticism of learners who may be disinterested in methods training into an asset.

The papers present the background, approaches and attitudes of learners as one of the common challenges for trainers. Corti and Van den Eynden (2015) discuss the teaching and learning of data management skills, both quantitative and qualitative, among learners from a spectrum of seniority, professional, and disciplinary backgrounds. They advocate flexible training which encourages 'learning by doing'. While learner diversity is to a greater or lesser extent apparent across the papers, in compulsory methods modules teachers face a further pressure of many students lacking interest or motivation. Scott Jones and Goldring (2015) demonstrate that this lack of interest may also be seen in teaching staff who perceive the conditions for their own methods learning and teaching as equally ghettoised and seemingly unrewarded as it appears to some students.

Importantly, this special issue does not stop at identifying challenges. Rather, it also contributes to pedagogic knowledge by providing detailed examples of engaging and motivating students through changes to pedagogic practice. Howard and Brady (2015) address the challenges of disinterested politics students, highlighting the mismatch between methods teaching and the largely post-structuralist emphasis in the rest of their substantive courses. They describe a constructivist pedagogical strategy whereby they enable and encourage students to construct their own learning experiences. Buckley et al. (2015) address the perceived irrelevance of methods teaching by embedding quantitative methods within substantive modules, moving from a transmissionist to a connectionist approach. In doing so they simultaneously support students to apply quantitative methods to substantive research questions of relevance to them, but also elevate the profile of methods teaching in the department.

The special issue addresses the use of computer software for data analysis and the implications for learners and teachers in relation to both quantitative and qualitative methods. Buckley et al. (2015) and Scott Jones and Goldring (2015) are concerned that quantitative software can become seen as the concept or construct, rather than the tool. Their pedagogical problem solving involves helping learners to go further and gain a deeper understanding of the methodological issues rather than software procedures. Silver and Woolf (2015) describe the challenge of teaching CAQDAS, emphasising facilitation over instruction to support learners to harness and apply the potential of CAQDAS to their own research tasks. They present a pedagogic approach whereby teachers can orientate themselves with learners' research requirements by guiding them in 'translating' their knowledge from broad 'tactics' to practicable 'strategies' for achieving their research goals.

The special issue, then, takes the reader into the realms of the pedagogical knowledge and decision-making of methods teachers who are working to engage constructively with the challenges before them. These teachers address challenges that are common to any teaching context plus those that are particular to, or particularly emphasised within, the context of building methodological capacity and literacy. Working more often with resources within their teams than from pedagogic theory or research evidence, the reflective practitioners are producing their own grass roots solutions to lived problems. The issue generates a picture of praxis: the 'wise and prudent practical judgement about how to act in *this* situation' (Carr & Kemmis, 1986, p. 190) of a variety of methods teacher-practitioner-researchers. Collectively the authors contribute to the much-needed task of building the pedagogic culture around research methods.

Note

1. We are grateful to the following who have reviewed papers for this special issue. Anna Bagnoli, University of Cambridge, UK. Joanna Ball, University of Sussex, UK. Jenny Byrne, University of Southampton, UK. Christian Bokhove, University of Southampton, UK. Emily Clough, Newcastle University, UK. Amos Channon, University of Southampton, UK. Amanda Coffey, Cardiff University, UK. Alicia Curtin, University College, Cork, Ireland. Peter Davis, Auckland, New Zealand. Heather Elliott, Institute of Education, London, UK. Louise Gazeley, University of Sussex, UK. Martyn Hammersley, The Open University, UK. Matt Homer, University of Leeds, UK. Maggie Kubanyiova, University of Birmingham, UK. Pauline Leonard, University of Southampton, UK. Jo Rose, University of Bristol, UK. Jane Seale, University of Exeter, UK. Luke Sloan, Cardiff University, UK. Paul Stoneman, University of Surrey, UK. Liz Todd, Newcastle University, UK. Mark Vicars, Victoria University, Australia. Pamela Woolner, Newcastle University, UK.

References

Adriaensen, J., Kerremans, B., & Slootmaeckers, K. (2015). Editors' introduction to the thematic issue: Mad about methods? Teaching research methods in political science. *Journal of Political Science Education, 11*(1), 1–10. doi:10.1080/15512169.2014.985017

BIS. (2014). *The allocation of science and research funding, 2015/16: Investing in world-class science and research*. London: Department for Business, Innovation and Skills.

Bishop, L. (2012). Using archived qualitative data for teaching: Practical and ethical considerations. *International Journal of Social Research Methodology, 15*, 341–350. doi:10.1080/13645579.2012.688335

Buckley, J., Brown, M., Thomson, S., Olsen, W., & Carter, J. (2015). Embedding quantitative skills into the Social Science curriculum: Case studies from Manchester. *International Journal of Social Research Methodology, 18*, 495–510.

Bulmer, M. (1985). The development of sociology and of empirical social research in Britain. In M. Bulmer (Ed.), *Essays on the history of British sociological research* (pp. 3–37). Cambridge: Cambridge University Press.

Carr, W., & Kemmis, S. (1986). *Becoming critical: Education, knowledge and action research*. Lewes: Falmer.

Corti, L. & Van den Eynden, V. (2015). Learning to manage and share data: Jump-starting the research methods curriculum. *International Journal of Social Research Methodology, 18*, 545–559.

Earley, M. (2014). A synthesis of the literature on research methods education. *Teaching in Higher Education, 19*, 242–253. doi:10.1080/13562517.2013.860105

Garner, M., Wagner, C., & Kawulich, B. (2009). *Teaching research methods in the social sciences*. Farnham: Ashgate Publishing Group.

HEA. (2015). *Social sciences blog: Teaching research methods in the social sciences*. Retrieved from http://blogs.heacademy.ac.uk/social-sciences/category/teaching-research-methods/

Hernández-Hernández, F., & Sancho-Gil, J. (in press). A learning process within an education research group: An approach to learning qualitative research methods. *International Journal of Social Research Methodology*.

Howard, C. & Brady, M. (2015). Teaching social research methods after the critical turn: Challenges and benefits of a constructivist pedagogy. *International Journal of Social Research Methodology, 18*, 511–525.

Hesse-Biber, S. (2015). The problems and prospects in the teaching of mixed methods research. *International Journal of Social Research Methodology, 18*, 463–477.

Hurworth, R. (2008). *Teaching qualitative research: Cases and issues*. Rotterdam: Sense.

Kilburn, D., Nind, M., & Wiles, R. (2014a). Learning as researchers and teachers: The development of a pedagogical culture for social science research methods? *British Journal of Educational Studies, 62*, 191–207.

Kilburn, D., Nind, M., & Wiles, R. (2014b). *Short courses in advanced research methods: Challenges and opportunities for teaching and learning*. National Centre for Research Methods (NCRM) Report. Retrieved from http://eprints.ncrm.ac.uk/3601/

Kottmann, A. (2011). Reform of doctoral training in Europe: A silent revolution? In J. Enders, H. de Boer, & D. Westerheijden (Eds.), *Reform of higher education in Europe* (pp. 29–43). Rotterdam: Sense.

Loxley, A., Seery, A., & Grenfell, M. (2013). Editorial: Teaching and learning research methodology. *International Journal of Research & Method in Education, 36*, 209–212. doi:10.1080/1743727X.2013.819704

Moley, S., Wiles, R., & Sturgis, P. (2013). *Advanced research methods training in the UK: Current provision and future strategies*. Project Report. Southampton: National Centre for Research Methods. Unpublished.

Nind, M., Curtin, A., & Hall, K. (in press). *Research methods for pedagogy*. London: Bloomsbury.

Nind, M., Kilburn, D., & Wiles, R. (2014). *The teaching of research methods: Fostering discursive pedagogic spaces in capacity building*. Porto: European Conference of Educational Research.

Nind, M., Kilburn, D., & Wiles, R. (2015). Using video and dialogue to generate pedagogic knowledge: Teachers, learners and researchers reflecting together on the pedagogy of social research methods. *International Journal of Social Research Methodology, 18*, 561–576.

Payne, G., & Williams, M. (Eds.). (2011). *Teaching quantitative methods: Getting the basics right*. London: Sage.

Peden, B., & Carroll, D. (2009). Historical trends in teaching research methods by psychologists in the United States. In M. Garner, C. Wagner, & B. Kawulich (Eds.), *Teaching research methods in the social sciences* (pp. 23–35). Farnham: Ashgate Publishing Group.

Scott Jones, J., & Goldring, J. E. (2015). I'm not a quants person'; Key strategies in building competence and confidence in staff who teach quantitative research methods. *International Journal of Social Research Methodology, 18*.

Silver, C., & Woolf, N. H. (2015). From guided-instruction to facilitation of learning: The development of Five-level QDA as a CAQDAS pedagogy that explicates the practices of expert users. *International Journal of Social Research Methodology, 18*, 527–543.

Wagner, C., Garner, M., & Kawulich, B. (2011). The state of the art of teaching research methods in the social sciences: Towards a pedagogical culture. *Studies in Higher Education, 36*, 75–88. doi:10.1080/03075070903452594

Melanie Nind
National Centre for Research Methods, University of Southampton
Southampton, UK

Daniel Kilburn
University College London, London, UK

Rebekah Luff
National Centre for Research Methods, University of Southampton
Southampton, UK

The problems and prospects in the teaching of mixed methods research

Sharlene Hesse-Biber

Department of Sociology, Boston College, Chestnut Hill, MA, USA

> There are pedagogical challenges USA students and instructors face within mixed methods classrooms. Instructors of mixed methods are often self-taught, lacking adequate training in both qualitative and quantitative approaches to research. Students are not often trained in both research approaches. These dual training gaps can result in deep pedagogical issues compromising students' ability to fully understand mixed methods research praxis and leaving teachers feeling ill equipped to address students' learning concerns. To tackle the myriad of challenges confronted in the mixed methods classroom requires structural changes to the current way graduate training programs in social research methods are organized and taught. Developing a team-based teaching approach to mixed methods research that provides students with instructors who have the requisite qualitative and quantitative knowledge can serve as a pedagogical model that can begin at least to address the current methods and methodological skills gap in the teaching of mixed methods research.

Introduction

Mixed methods research courses in the United States are primarily offered at the graduate and upper-division undergraduate level, and have only emerged over the course of the last five years (Frels, Onwuegbuzie, Leech, & Collins, 2012). A recent study of one hundred schools of education throughout the USA notes that twenty-two percent of graduate programs require their graduate students to enroll in a mixed methods course. In addition, twenty percent of educational programs encourage students to take one mixed methods course as an elective offering (Leech & Goodwin, 2008). At the same time, there is a lack of pedagogical literature on the challenges of teaching students mixed methods (Onwuegbuzie, Frels, Leech, & Collins, 2011).

There is an overall deficit of a pedagogical culture with regard to teaching research methods in general. Wagner, Garner, and Kawulich (2011) conducted a systematic literature review of articles published between 1997 and 2007 concluding that there was little guidance provided to teachers of research methods. Earley's (2014) extensive review of the literature on this topic notes the paucity of pedagogical research on the problems and prospects regarding student learning of research methods. These studies also point out the lack of interdisciplinary context in the teaching of research methods as a whole.

Most faculty currently teaching mixed methods courses have not themselves taken such a course in their academic career. Creswell, Tashakkori, Jensen, and Shapley (2003, p. 620) refer to these individuals as the 'first generation of faculty' who more or less are teaching themselves the 'how-to's' of doing mixed methods research and at the same time trying out the 'how-to's' of teaching these methods to their students. Earley (2007, p. 146) notes that those who are the teaching pioneers of mixed methods courses, '... find ourselves in the same situation: we were not officially trained in the mixed-methods research process and have to create these courses without the benefit of prior coursework to guide us.' In addition, Frels et al. (2012) state that that few studies examine the issues students and instructors face in the contemporary mixed methods classroom thus leaving a pedagogical gap in our understanding of 'what works' well in the teaching and student learning in the mixed methods classroom.

Yet there are signals that the pedagogical ground is shifting toward an increased focus on teaching and learning of research methods as a whole. Kilburn, Nind, and Wiles (2014) path-breaking work on the pedagogical state of social science research methods in UK higher education included an in-depth exploration of twenty-four published papers that specifically addressed research methods 'pedagogical culture.' In analyzing these papers, the authors note the wealth and range of activities and formal classroom learning that is related to the building of students' skills in research methods. Their review of the resource rich content in these papers concludes on a more optimistic note and they discerned in their review, three important goals of an effective pedagogical process. The first goal is to make the learning of research visible through engaging students in a series of learning exercises across the research process. The second goal is to have students conduct their own research. The final goal is to have students critically reflect on their own research praxis.

Levine et al.'s (n.d.) work is one of the few studies to address some of the specific challenges students and instructors encounter in the mixed methods classroom. The authors, too, engaged in 'reflective learning' in their mixed methods course, which took the form of using students' weekly mixed methods classroom reflections as the basis of subsequent class discussion and debate. This served to specifically identify and address student-learning issues as they unfolded over the course of the semester. These 'reflective' learning discussions served at times to clear up some crucial issues students were encountering. The authors note that they dealt with 'grey area' studies where the qualitative component was usually not developed fully. One finding that came out of the analysis of their data was the presence of 'persistent issues,' such as how to address student issues with regard to analyzing mixed methods data. This type of reflective pedagogy they present has many of the elements of the effective pedagogical process uncovered by Kilburn et al. (2014).

As mixed methods continues to become a growing field in social research, it is critical for faculty who are teaching, or who are contemplating teaching, mixed methods to understand the methodological and methods challenges students learning about mixed methods confront as they begin to tackle the complexity of mixing and analyzing research findings from two different methods and often from multiple theoretical perspectives.

Toward a mixed methods pedagogy

I recently taught two graduate seminars on mixed methods research inquiry. I decided to teach this course in an iterative manner, somewhat like the 'reflexive discussions' that Levine et al. (n.d.) engaged in when they taught their mixed methods course. Right from the beginning I encouraged students to keep a log of their experiences in learning about mixing methods and the concerns and issues they were having in understanding the nuts and bolts of mixing methods. I specifically asked students to clarify for me at the beginning of each class what they perceived as some critical points of confusion about just what mixed methods entails and what they found most difficult.

Most of the graduate students in my mixed methods courses were at a midpoint in their graduate career and many were at the pre-dissertation or dissertation proposal writing stage, with most of their course work completed. They hailed from different professional schools and most were getting an applied professional advanced degree in the healthcare field. The prerequisite for enrollment in my mixed methods course required students to have taken at least one graduate research methods course. As the semester progressed, it became clear to me that students taking my course, for the most part, had education and training in only one type of method – either qualitative or quantitative – that was housed within their discipline.

Student challenges in the learning of mixed methods

Many students came to a mixed methods course not sure of just what it would mean for them to learn a new methods approach and then proceed to engage with both qualitative and quantitative approaches in one research project. It was clear to them that adding a new method would often require them to switch their disciplinary mental model and research practices, and this was not something many of them anticipated, understood, or were prepared for.

It was not surprising that when I asked students in my mixed methods course what they found the most difficult thing about learning mixed methods, they all seem to agree on the following point: mixing paradigms brought confusion. Their own methods training gave them little understanding of how qualitative and quantitative methods were connected to a set of philosophical assumptions about the nature of the social world. The course readings they encountered during the first two weeks of the mixed methods course maintained a tight link between theory and method, with a discussion of the range of different paradigmatic stances toward knowledge building that spanned the qualitative and qualitative divide. Learning about paradigmatic viewpoints raised issues that touched on whether or not paradigms could be mixed within *one* mixed methods study.

The following are some examples of what students relayed to me when I asked them more specifically about their understanding of what it meant to have a paradigmatic point of view. It is important to note the differences in their responses depending upon whether they came from a predominantly qualitative or quantitative background.

One graduate student with a quantitative background in the field of education said: 'I didn't know I had a paradigm!' Another student in the health sciences noted:

> Positivism in my field is so 'secure' that is not something I have considered before in terms of what this means for me individually and how this stance has influenced my

research endeavors, particularly the development of my dissertation (which is in a quantitative data collection stage currently).

Another student with a strong social justice qualitative background noted the following:

> I'd like to focus in this note on one strong bias that I have at the research design phase. I'm biased towards research that injects the voices, opinions, and ideas of marginalized populations into the halls of power. Another bias is to privilege those populations' viewpoints over those of so-called experts. Often times those marginalized populations are the ones that have suffered the most from a discriminatory governmental policy, a brutal war, etc. They are often also the ones who have the most to gain from a remedy. Moreover, they are often the ones who have the least say over policy decisions moving forward. I suppose I view this bias as a sort of affirmative action. As such, it is an innate bias and one that I try to continue imposing on my research.

Once students began to uncover their own biases, and started to be open to the idea of a range of paradigmatic stances a researcher might take when considering a mixed methods approach, their concerns shifted to issues of paradigm incompatibility. One student expressed the following concern with regard to this issue: 'Which paradigm are we situated in, how is it possible to exist in both paradigms if they are opposing, can we mix these paradigms and conduct a mixed methods research study, and which set of rules will our study be held to?'

Another source of confusion for students centered on what a mixed methods question was. One student quoted in the Levine et al. study noted:

> I'm still struggling to nail down my research question – I know the different quantitative and qualitative components, but I'm trying to find a good way to merge them under a broader objective. Regardless, it was great to work through the different components with my peers.

When asking mixed methods questions, students were curious about just how paradigms fit into the asking of a mixed methods question. Their queries about this took the following form: Can an interpretive paradigm include quantitative methods? Can quantitative paradigms include qualitative methods? One student mentioned that she could not imagine creating a research question that would include both a qualitative and quantitative paradigm.

Another source of confusion for students centered on how they should go about analyzing mixed methods data. They wanted to know how two very different data forms could connect to one another. Students' knowledge of different analytical methods was sparse. Quantitatively trained students usually had only one statistical analysis and a few had taken one advanced statistical course. Most qualitatively trained students had taken an introductory graduate qualitative course that focused on either field work/ethnography or interviewing. The most common type of analysis they used was grounded theory, but they were hard-pressed to tell me more about the type of grounded theory they employed. They also mentioned that they did not have much hands-on experience using this analytical tool. Students asked me some of the following types of questions: Can quantitative research findings ever be connected to or related to qualitative findings? How? It seems in some studies that qualitative research is always being conducted as secondary to the quantitative – Why? Is not qualitative research sometimes needed in order to even determine quantitative research component and its question? As I listened to the types of methods training students received, it became clear that it was hard for them to tackle deploying one data collection method and analytical tool to their research project. In addition, students mentioned that they had little training in foundational issues and how they entered the research process.

During the course of learning about different paradigmatic approaches in my course, students also began to question their own paradigmatic stance toward mixed methods projects. Students often asked me how their own paradigmatic stance might begin to cloud their own thinking about how to proceed with a mixed methods project, asking questions such as: Is my going into mixed methods research with a firm ideology and failing to move from that ideology, particularly if it is from a positivist paradigm, the best way to conduct mixed methods research project?

Given these sources of confusion, one important first challenge in the teaching of mixed methods involves moving students from either a deductive mode of research inquiry to an *inductive* one, or vice versa. This type of transition in knowledge building requires a discussion of paradigmatic viewpoints linked to research questions that are then linked to methods selected. I ask my students questions such as the following: What does it mean to ask a deductive question? What does it mean to take an inductive approach? What is an inductive question? How are these two modes of knowledge building linked? I provide students with specific examples and empirical research studies that ask questions using both types of research inquiry. I have found that the use of concrete short case studies to invaluable in the learning process.

As students proceed to transition to other ways of knowing, students often find themselves asking a series of philosophical questions that often start to upend their former ways of thinking about research inquiry. Instructors of mixed methods must have the knowledge and training in both modes of knowledge building in order to transition students to thinking along a theory-question-methods continuum. If not, students may not fully understand or even begin to appreciate the profound links between theory and research design as a whole.

Teaching mixed methods: what works, what confusion still remains and acknowledgment of reflexivity

I often start out my mixed methods course by getting a sense of a student's prior methods and theory training. As I mentioned, the pre-requisite for entering this course is having at least one general graduate methods course, and so I begin by asking students to tell me about their own researcher positionality. I ask them to write down the general types of questions they tended to ask in their own past research projects and what specific methods and theories lie in their theory/methods comfort zone.

I then discuss the importance of knowing what specific values/attitudes/perspectives they apply in their own research projects. The importance of being conscious of their researcher standpoint is one way to offset researcher bias within their research projects. I then discuss the importance of being reflexive throughout the research process, drawing on my training in feminist approaches to research inquiry (Hesse-Biber, 2014). I note that being reflexive means to interrogate one's values and attitudes by recognizing that 'all knowledge is affected by the social conditions under which it is produced and that it is grounded in both the social location and the social biography of the observer and the observed' (Mann & Kelley, 1997, p. 392).

A useful pedagogical tool to practice reflexivity in the mixed methods class is the following reflexive exercise that I use in all my methods courses. I ask each student at the beginning of the course to take 20 min to write down what they perceive to be the values and attitudes they hold that impact the ways in which they go about approaching a research project, specifically asking them to answer the following questions:

What particular biases, if any, do I bring to and/or impose onto my research?

How do my specific values and attitudes and theoretical perspectives influence the research style you take on? How do my values and attitudes and beliefs enter into the research process? Do I only ask questions from my perspective?

How does my own agenda shape what ask and what I find?

How does my positionality impact how I gather, analyze, and interpret my data: From whose perspective?

After completing this exercise students share what they feel comfortable sharing in small class discussions. I also ask students to keep a research journal in which they reflect on their own research conundrums and ephanies throughout the mixed methods course. This can be quite helpful to students as they evaluate their own experiences in learning mixed methods. One female graduate student in social work responded to the exercise by noting:

While I would like to consider myself unbiased, I believe the reality is that we are all biased to some extent based on past experiences, education, personal beliefs, cultural exposure, worldviews, etc. The primary bias that I am trying to undo is the one inculcated in myself through my education regarding the preeminence of positivist and objectivist quantitative research and theory development over qualitative methods and more subjective methodologies.

There are a range of important sources of confusion students confront as they proceed in learning about mixed methods. Many of the students in the class have only had training in one type of method and methodology. With the exception of one student, most of the students in the class had training in quantitative methods with a post-positivist theoretical lens. The first part of the course introduces students to a range of paradigmatic points of view onto the social world and discusses the questions that often flow from a given paradigmatic stance. For some students this is the first time that they were consciously aware that they were seeped in a given paradigm – that of post-positivism. Once conscious of their own paradigmatic world-view, they began to ask how mixing methods of different types would be linked to a given paradigm and could they use post-positivism for both methods and so forth. One student asked:

What if one undertakes a mixed method study from say a post-positivistic stance? Does the qualitative component then become post-positivistic as well and therefore separated from its own methodological, ontological, and epistemological assumptions in its service to the quantitative essence?

In discussing paradigmatic assumptions, I tie this discussion to the specific types of research questions students' address in their own research. I often start out asking students about what questions lend them to a qualitative approach? A quantitative approach? We discuss the differences between the two types of question asking modes (confirmatory questions versus exploratory questions). I then link these different types of questions to a discussion of the assumptions each question makes about the nature of the social world – what can be known? Who can know? And so on.

Envisioning the mixed methods research process

I then proceed to ask the students what they think a mixed methods question might look like. This form of inquiry usually leads to more confusion in that students are not clear about what a mixed methods question would look like. Here, I rely heavily on case studies that deploy a variety of different qualitatively driven and quantitatively driven mixed methods questions. We also explore the situation where the types of questions asked take a different approach, but their goals are to tackle the same research problem with the goal of coming up with a similar set of findings in the serve of providing a more valid set of findings.

In general, students understand that a mixed methods question encompasses different types of research questions in one study. These questions are not mixed, but they can serve many different objectives depending on the overall goals of the research study. I found that students came to appreciate that the overall research objectives will dictate how each question is positioned in the research project. Through interrogating specific empirical case studies, students were able to examine exemplary mixed methods projects from a quantitatively-driven/qualitatively-driven and triangulation perspective.

In discussing the different types of mixed methods questions, I also stress how each question asked is linked to a specific method or set of methods. I ask my students about what types of mixed methods design would serve to answer the range of research questions. I ask them to reflect on how mixed methods questions relate to one another: To what extent if any if one question more dominant in the project, and if so, what role does the other question place? How are the methods linked to those questions and in turn how do the findings gathered from the asking of question relate?

It is at this juncture that my mixed methods class segues from issue of data collection to the topic of analysis and interpretation of mixed methods data – more specifically, to addressing how the data collected from two different mixed methods components can be analyzed. It is important to note here that this very issue also plagues the mixed methods research community as a whole.

The field of mixed methods itself finds this particular question difficult to answer and the ways forward are not often clear. I think it is important to share with students the issues that still remain in a growing field of praxis like mixed methods inquiry. Namely, what does one do with data gathered across qualitative and quantitative approaches? How does a quantitatively-driven researcher, for example, assess the importance and meaning of the qualitative data collected when they may not have training in assessing how to do this and vice versa? What should be the overall goal in the analysis of different data types? Should they be integrated? How? Should they be separate analyses?

As I begin this phase of the course, a new set of questions comes to the surface as students grapple with the case studies and their analytical and interpretive practices. One student in my class, who was trained as a quantitatively driven researcher, asked me whether the qualitative component she used in her mixed methods study would then become post-positivistic as well. If this was so, she went on to ask me how quantitative research could ever build off qualitative finding. Another student was concerned about what he saw as the delegation of qualitative methods to a secondary position in the research articles he had read. He asked me, 'Must qualitative research always be done as an auxiliary to quantitative? Is not qualitative research sometimes needed in order to determine quantitative research aims?'

To begin to answer these questions, I have students read a variety of short empirical case study articles that use different types of sequential mixed methods research designs, starting with qualitatively and quantitatively driven mixed methods designs. I then have them look at the range of different analytical and interpretative choices that are dictated by how the researcher positions each component and its specific role in the research process. I also use case studies that deploy concurrent (triangulated designs and nested) mixed methods designs. I point out to my students that in undertaking a mixed methods project, it is important to possess a range of analytical and interpretative lenses and tools, as well as a profound appreciation for the potential contributions a given methodological perspective can bring to a mixed methods project. A respect for methodological, methods, analytical, and interpretative differences is a critical ingredient to successful mixed methods praxis.

I also tell my students that many projects that authors claim to be mixed methods still remain unmixed, with little interaction between the two methods (Bryman, 2006b, 2007; Yin, 2006). In effect, we are still witnessing the publication of parallel quantitative and quantitative components (for a discussion of these issues, see Bazeley, 2003; Bryman, 2006a, 2007; Hesse-Biber, 2010; O'Cathain, Murphy, & Nicholl, 2007; O'Cathain, Nicholl, & Murphy, 2009).

Engaging with this type of mixed methods analysis and interpretation phase then also requires researchers to come out of their methods and theoretical comfort zones. This is often a process in which the research becomes both an insider and an outsider, taking on multiple standpoints and negotiating different researcher identities simultaneously. These are indeed critical mixed methods praxis issues that are not easy to address in the mixed methods classroom, as it requires my students to also obtain the theoretical skills and analytical methods they may not yet have. This cannot be easily obtained in just one class period.

Highlighting the importance of a research question and how it is linked to method, analysis and interpretation

I begin to chip away at this analytical/interpretative conundrum by reminding my students that it is important at the analysis and interpretation stage in a mixed methods research design to be aware of the question that each data collection component is answering. What does each design component play in the analysis and interpretation? It is also important to understand that each question is also rooted in particular research methodology – that has its particular set of assumptions about the social world. Brannen and O'Connell (2015) work on doing mixed methods analysis provides some important strategies for thinking about the data analysis, interpretation and writing up stage of a mixed methods project. In interpreting and writing up your mixed methods findings they stress the importance of taking a 'narrative approach,' whereby the researcher addresses the various ways each of the data set's findings inform each other both alone and using them together. Another critical insight these authors suggest addressing first and foremost is that each of the findings using a different method do not necessarily have to agree with one another, as in a mixed methods traditional triangulated design. Instead, each study's findings can complement or provide a more complex understanding of the problem being addressed.

What is clear from the research into barriers of integrating mixed methods research findings is that there is a skills gap among those conducting mixed methods research that may require the addition of new analytical options for assessing how different data forms can connect to one another. These analytical options are still emerging among those members who are traversing this landscape.

The movement toward a mixed methods pedagogy culture

The experience of teaching mixed methods in the graduate classroom and some of the issues/barriers and glimmers of hope I have experienced, lead me back to the recent findings garnered from Kilburn et al.'s (2014) pedagogical dimensions that facilitate student learning of research methods in general. I concur with their pedagogical goal of student-centered learning. My pedagogical experience in the mixed methods classroom has been that the students need to be engaged with the learning of research methods. It is critical to present provide them with a range of hands-on activities that allow them to take learning risks; to apply the more abstract ideas they have learn in a more formal way. Along with this goal is to provide classroom space for a more back and forth reflexive learning dimension. It is critical for students to share what they have found hard or difficult in the application of more formal methods concepts in carrying out mixed methods research activities. What is also critical especially within the context of teaching mixed methods is what Kilburn et al. (2014) note as the engaging of students in interdisciplinary moments of interaction within the methods classroom and the encouragement of dialogue across what to many of them have heretofore been research/disciplinary research paradigmatic divides. Likewise, there must be a pedagogical space for teachers of mixed methods to engage in dialogue about their own pedagogical concerns and issues and the ability to share resources and new ideas that continue to foster a mixed methods pedagogical culture.

The good news is that there is an emergence of new paths along the mixed methods analytical terrain, as demonstrated by the development of a range of emergent analytical mixed methods frameworks for integrating both qualitative and quantitative data (see Brannen & O'Connell, 2015). These analytical developments open up new analytical ground for moving mixed methods analysis and interpretation beyond a parallel analytical approach. One such example is that of data transformation (i.e. the process of qualitizing and quantitizing; see, e.g. Sandelowski, Voils, & Knafl, 2009). In addition, computer-assisted data analysis programs now include a mixed methods component to facilitate complex analyses of mixed methods data (Bazeley, 2003).

In my teaching of mixed methods at the graduate level, I found that one of the best strategies for demonstrating analysis and interpretation of mixed methods data is to again provide students with exemplary mixed methods case studies of how this has been done successfully, and talking through the specific step-by-step analytical approach each researcher took along the way to accomplish this type of analysis and interpretation of their multiple data sets. We discuss the issue of just how the two data sets can 'talk' to one another and what role each plays – the questions each data-set answers and how each contributes to the overall research project objectives. A case study by Moffatt, White, Mackingtosh, and Howel (2006) is an excellent example of how this can be done. The study is based on a pilot randomized controlled trial (RCT) of individuals above age sixty and was designed to determine the impact of providing welfare rights advice within primary care setting in the UK. The authors' goal was to show how such interventions could tackle age-based health inequities. The study used a concurrent mixed methods longitudinal design consisting of a quantitative and qualitative component. Quantitative data was gathered from a random sample of 126 participants (119 at final follow-up) who were invited from the databases of four general practices in the 'most deprived wards' of Newcastle upon Tyne. Quantitative data was gathered from structured surveys (four over two years) that used a variety of standard psychological scales that measured participants' mental health – their levels of anxiety and depression – as well as covering the areas of demographics and physical health. A sub-sample of survey participants was then recruited for the qualitative interview component. Each participant in the qualitative sub-sample component was interviewed twice; 25 participants at baseline and 22 participants 12–18 months later. The interviews covered a range of topics that centered on participants' lived experiences regarding the impact of resources (material and financial) on their physical and mental health, as well as their assessment of the impacts of the overall study intervention. All participants were then randomized into 'control' and 'intervention' groups.

The quantitative data showed no statistically significant impact of interventions on health and social outcomes. However, the qualitative interviews revealed that despite this, every interviewee saw their intervention as positive. Every participant also felt that negative health outcomes were a result of age, family history, fate, or other factors that could not be affected by extra money or resources. Extra money would only serve to improve other facets of their lives. While the quantitative and qualitative data appeared to be in conflict, the researchers sought to resolve these divergences in their concurrent data sets. They did so by placing both data sets in conversation with one another by recognizing the fundamental differences between quantitative and qualitative components' questions and findings. Each component was tapping into a set of different questions. The authors came to appreciate the complementarity of their data even if the questions were not exactly the same. Moffatt et al. also looked at the methodological rigor of each component, comparing the samples, and collected further data for verification, and addressing unexpected factors that would affect the data, and comparing the outcomes to find use of both complementary and contradictory findings. Although a positivist theoretical lens is the dominant paradigm in RCT, the authors argue that the infusion of a qualitative subjective component into RCTs can serve to strengthen and enhance the overall interpretation of RCT findings.

After going through the entire research design outcomes of the Moffat et al. study, I ask students to complete the following exercise. I have them work in pairs as a way to allow each student to articulate and reflect with one another regarding their respective analytical rationales with regard to the following specific analysis questions:

(1) What is Moffatt et al.'s overall research question or set of questions they want to answer?
(2) Draw a diagram of Moffatt et al.'s mixed methods research design. Construct a research design that accounts for the characteristics of mixed methods research as related in this article.

(3) Does each component of the research design answer the same or a different research question? Be specific.
(4) Why do the authors elect to add a subjective qualitative component to the RCT? In what sense, if any, does the introduction of a qualitative component add value to this study?
(5) What are the strengths and weaknesses (if any) of adding a qualitative component?
(6) Data analysis and interpretation: Describe the data analysis and interpretation stage of this mixed methods project. In your answer, please determine and explain how these authors decided on 'how and at what stage does mixing occur' if at all in this study. Describe the analysis of the qualitative and quantitative data. Were they mixed? Why or why not? How was each data-set validated?
(7) At this juncture, the researchers could have followed up their findings using another method of data collection. Would you recommend that they do so? Why or why not? What would be the goal of adding another methods component? What question would that new methods component answer or clarify?

Another critical conundrum students confront is how they can navigate constructing a mixed methods research proposal. Very often, students find that they lack specific guidelines in writing up their mixed methods proposal while their own disciplines have specific guidelines about how to format a dissertation proposal, mentioning nothing about mixed methods proposals. In addition, some of my students who have gone on to write a mixed methods dissertation proposal tell me that they cannot find committee members who are familiar with just what mixed methods is. They frequently find the need to bring in a faculty member from a different discipline who has knowledge and who has, in fact, conducted mixed methods research projects.

Students who wanted to explore doing a mixed methods project also wanted to know more about the specific issues they might confront, like how much time it would take them to complete a mixed methods dissertation. A student noted that she was fearful of being overwhelmed and puts it this way:

> I might become overwhelmed at the prospect of carrying out what could amount to multiple research projects with advising faculty who may not have the prerequisite knowledge on mixed methods research that could help see the dissertation to a timely completion. The situation may be that an advisor has experience with other forms of mixed methods research than the one chosen by the student, or has a different paradigmatic emphasis than that of the student.

As I discussed these issues with my class, we brainstormed about the possibility of choosing a range of advisors across departments who might have the different skill sets and theoretical lenses that would allow them to obtain the guidance they needed. We also talked about the difficulties in working with an interdisciplinary committee and all that issues that might entail in terms of faculty from difference disciplines trying to communicate across their own research divides. Students offered suggestions for novice and seasoned instructors of graduate research methods courses as a whole, especially with regard to the teaching of mixed methods. There are a few excellent resources I provide my students with regard to the specifics involved in preparing a mixed methods dissertation proposal. I have found Talab's (2009) online resource (http://coe.k-state.edu/annex/ecdol/MIxed_Methods. htm) to be a great tool for novice mixed methods researchers. One important pedagogical area that is ripe for integrating into the learning of mixed methods is the incorporation of some on-line mixed methods webinars and You-Tube clips that already exist that cover a range mixed methods topics. However, the quality and validity of these resources needs to be systematically reviewed. A mixed methods guide to such on-line resources might be a great contribution to facilitating a mixed methods pedagogy culture as well.

Future directions

In my teaching of mixed methods, I found that students desired even more guidelines and examples of the various ways mixed methods researchers use a range of mixed methods designs when tackling a given research problem. They wanted even more emphasis placed on learning about different paradigms and their linkages to research questions and methods not just in my course, but within their doctoral training as a whole. They also sought additional in-class exercises that specifically engaged them with different ways qualitative and quantitative findings 'interact' or inform one another through examining and walking-through the steps researchers took to complete their mixed methods journal articles. Students also sought more support and guidance from their disciplinary department. Students wanted more of their disciplinary faculty to receive specific training in conducting and teaching mixed methods research so that they could rely on faculty expertise within their home discipline as they began to write up their mixed methods proposals.

Given my own teaching of mixed methods over several years, I want to stress again the importance of taking a hands-on approach – providing students with in-class exercises around the thorny issues about learning mixed methods that I have discussed. I have found that using the power of peer group learning was effective in small groups in class discussions where students could share their own strategies, and share and reflect together on their own learning of mixed methods issues and successes. It is also important for instructors to develop an iterative reflexive model of getting feedback from students early and often as the mixed methods course proceeds. Levine et al. (n.d.) stress this as well, in order to deal with what they term the 'gray areas' of learning about mixed methods research.

The lack of training of faculty teaching mixed methods courses

Teaching a mixed methods course is a daunting task from the standpoint of the instructor. What is most crucial to make this type of teaching successful is for all instructors of mixed methods to possess extensive training in both theory and methods. In addition, it is important for instructors to have the experience of conducting their own mixed methods research projects that provide them with conducting mixed methods research, utilizing the range of designs and having the experience of grappling with the very issues my students bring to their mixed methods course.

What I fear most is having instructors teaching mixed methods that only have one type of training and theoretical skill set. Tashakkori and Teddlie (2003) early on pointed out that the continued polarization in the USA between qualitative and quantitative approaches has created a strong fissure in the teaching of research methods here such that students learn either from a qualitative or a quantitative approach and are often effectively forced to choose one type of approach. However, given the pressures to learn both methods approaches and the increasing popularity of a mixed methods approach, students need to learn how to navigate between these two approaches. An instructor, for example, who is trained primarily as a quantitative researcher with a post-positivist lens, needs to acquire a new theory/skills set before entering the mixed methods classroom. If not, how well will the qualitative component of the mixed methods design be brought into view in a mixed methods course? Will the qualitative component be just an add-on? Looking over the range of quantitatively driven mixed methods articles, one often discerns a type of superficial adding-on of the qualitative component whereby the qualitative findings amount to cherry picking quotes, for example, from interviews that support researchers' quantitative results. Such a rendering of what a qualitative approach is (method alone) without its methodological and analytical underpinnings does not make for a robust mixed methods research project. At worst it misinforms students about just what a qualitative approach is all about.

A multitude of pedagogical challenges lie ahead in the teaching of mixed methods. At this point there are few instructors within the social research methods community who possess the theory/methods skills to teach such a course effectively. The inclusion of multidisciplinary team-based teaching is necessary to move the teaching of mixed methods research forward and effectively produce the next generation of mixed methods teachers. One important element of a team-based pedagogical approach might be to model for students how research teams actually negotiate their standpoints with each other – demonstrating for students the often hidden types of 'give and take' praxis among interdisciplinary team members. Such an enactment can provide students with strategies for how to cross-disciplinary divides, methodological divides as well as methods divides productively. To begin to accomplish this, instructors themselves need to be open to new ways of knowing and, perhaps, have already acquired some experience in working within a team-based research environment, such that they themselves are open to new ways of knowing and have already crossed some different divides in terms of their own research standpoint. Instructors might begin to relate their own narratives on their own set of strategies they have found useful in this regard.

Structural barriers to mixed methods research that remain within and outside the academy

Much work remains to be done in order to pave the way for our students to effectively engage with mixed methods training and conduct mixed methods research projects within their disciplines. As already noted at the disciplinary/department level, students confront structural constraints with regard to writing up a mixed methods proposal and finding faculty within their own discipline that can teach and/or advise them. Even when they compete their research, they will confront a culture of journal publishing that is also divided along a qualitative/quantitative trajectory and that may be unwilling to be open to a mixed methods perspective, except for a select few journals that are specifically targeted as mixed methods journals. Even if a journal is open to a mixed methods research study, the effective writing-up a mixed methods project and doing this effectively may require an article word count that is over what the journal guidelines require. In fact, many journals have cut back their word counts for research articles. This trend, if it continues, will stifle the publishing of mixed methods research work and/or demand that researchers cut back on their methods and findings section in their publications.

Uncovering some of the challenging pedagogical issues and those promising strategies for addressing them is a good beginning. However, addressing the long-term structural issues – the methods and theory gaps in that exists among faculty and students – requires deep-rooted changes at the departmental and disciplinary level. This would involve looking at graduate training programs as a whole and a commitment of resources to re-tool graduate programs and the faculty training in interdisciplinary team-based research methods courses. This will also require a deep commitment of resources and a willingness of faculty to come out of their theory/methods comfort zones. It is important for instructors to engage with the differences they encounter by traversing the qualitative/quantitative divides they confront at multiple levels – the university and disciplinary – if we are to train the next generation of mixed methods researchers who can address a range of complex social problems. To do this well requires a commitment to also honor the collective contributions of a range of methodologies and methods.

These pedagogical dialogues within and across the disciplines needs to include team-based solutions that can serve to fill the methods and skills gap that currently exists in the teaching of social research methods, especially the teaching of mixed methods. Engaging in a deep dialogic process that is ongoing and open toward the inclusion of a diverse and multiple perspectives onto the effective teaching and learning of mixed methods can hold the promise of unleashing the synergistic potential of mixed methods research endeavors as a whole.

Disclosure statement

No potential conflict of interest was reported by the author.

References

Bazeley, P. (2003). Computerized data analysis for mixed methods research. In A. Tashakkori & C. Teddlie (Eds.), *Handbook of mixed methods in social & behavioral research* (pp. 385–422). Thousand Oaks, CA: Sage.

Brannen, J., & O'Connell, R. (2015). Data analysis: Overview of data analysis strategies. In S. Hesse-Biber & B. Johnson (Eds.), *Oxford handbook of multimethod and mixed methods research inquiry* (pp. 257–274). New York, NY: Oxford University Press.

Bryman, A. (2006a). Integrating quantitative and qualitative research: How is it done? *Qualitative Research, 6*, 97–113.

Bryman, A. (2006b). Paradigm peace and the implications for quality. *International Journal of Social Research Methodology, 9*, 111–126.

Bryman, A. (2007). Barriers to integrating quantitative and qualitative research. *Journal of Mixed Methods Research, 1*, 8–22.

Creswell, J. W., Tashakkori, A., Jensen, K. D., & Shapley, K. L. (2003). Teaching mixed methods research: Practices, dilemmas, and challenges. In A. Tashakkori & C. Teddlie (Eds.), *Handbook of mixed methods in social and behavioral research* (pp. 619–637). Thousand Oaks, CA: Sage.

Earley, M. A. (2007). Developing a syllabus for a mixed-methods research course. *International Journal of Social Research Methodology, 10*, 145–162.

Earley, M. (2014). A synthesis of the literature on research methods education. *Teaching in Higher Education, 19*, 242–253.

Frels, R. K., Onwuegbuzie, A. J., Leech, N. L., & Collins, K. T. (2012). Challenges to teaching mixed research courses. *Journal of Effective Teaching, 12*, 23–44.

Hesse-Biber, S. (2010). *Mixed methods research: Merging theory with practice*. New York, NY: Guilford Publications.

Hesse-Biber, S. (Ed.). (2014). *Feminist research practice: A primer*. Thousand Oaks, CA: Sage.

Kilburn, D., Nind, M., & Wiles, R. (2014). Learning as researchers and teachers: The development of a pedagogical culture for social science research methods? *British Journal of Educational Studies, 62*, 191–207. doi:10.1080/00071005.2014.918576

Leech, N. L., & Goodwin, L. D. (2008). Building a methodological foundation: Doctoral-level methods courses in colleges of education. *Research in the Schools, 15*(1), 1–8.

Levine, A., Nicolau, B., & Pluye, P. (n.d.). *Challenges in teaching mixed methods. Poster presentation*. McGill University, Montreal, Canada.

Mann, S. A., & Kelley, L. R. (1997). Standing at the crossroads of modernist thought: Collins, Smith, and the new feminist epistemologies. *Gender and Society, 11*, 391–408.

Moffatt, S., White, M., Mackingtosh, J., & Howel, D. (2006). Using quantitative and qualitative data in health services research – What happens when mixed methods findings conflict? *BMC Health Services Research, 6*. Retrieved from http://www.biomedcentral.com/1472-6963/6/28

O'Cathain, A., Murphy, E., & Nicholl, J. (2007). Integration and publications as indicators of "yield" from mixed methods studies. *Journal of Mixed Methods Research, 1*, 147–163.

O'Cathain, A., Nicholl, J., & Murphy, E. (2009). Structural issues affecting mixed methods studies in health research: A qualitative study. *BMC Medical Research Methodology, 9*, 82.

Onwuegbuzie, A. J., Frels, R. K., Leech, N. L., & Collins, K. M. T. (2011, February). *A mixed research study of approaches used by mixed research instructors*. Paper presented at the annual meeting of the Southwest Educational Research Association, San Antonio, TX.

Sandelowski, M., Voils, C. I., & Knafl, G. (2009). On quantitizing. *Journal of Mixed Methods Research, 3*, 208–222.

Talab, R. (2009, February). *Preparing a dissertation proposal: The mixed methods version*. Kansas State University. Retrieved from http://coe.kstate.edu/annex/ecdol/MIxed_Methods.htm

Tashakkori, A., & Teddlie, C. (2003). Issues and dilemmas in teaching research methods courses in social and behavioural sciences: US perspective. *International Journal of Social Research Methodology, 6*, 61–77.

Wagner, C., Garner, M., & Kawulich, B. (2011). The state of the art of teaching research methods in the social sciences: Towards a pedagogical culture. *Studies in Higher Education, 36*, 75–88.

Yin, R. K. (2006). Mixed methods research: Are the methods genuinely integrated or merely parallel? *Research in the Schools, 13*, 41–47.

'I'm not a quants person'; key strategies in building competence and confidence in staff who teach quantitative research methods'

Julie Scott Jones and John E. Goldring

Sociology, Manchester Metropolitan University, Manchester, UK

> Initiatives, like the UK ESRC's RDI/CI programmes and the Q-Step Centres, have a long-term aim of addressing the well-documented decline in the pool of academics able and willing to teach quantitative methods (QM). However, these initiatives will take time to make an impact; therefore, the upskilling of current staff is a vital strategy if we want to maintain QM in curricula. This paper draws on findings from the ESRC RDI project, 'No More Pointy Clicky, numbers stuff; building staff quantitative skills'. This project focussed on upskilling staff in a large Sociology department. The project was committed to delivering training to develop staff competence in QM; however, it became clear that this alone would not be sufficient to build staff confidence. Therefore, the project rolled-out a more complex strategy that addressed a range of central issues, including, pedagogy, infrastructure, Departmental resourcing and strategy, and staff worldviews, which this article explores.

Background – QM on the margins of British social science

The UK has one of the best-funded and largest, but underused, social science data infrastructures in the world. Its underuse is mainly due to the well documented decline in quantitative methods (henceforth QM) within UK Sociology, and a range of allied social sciences. A decline both as a component of university curricula and as empirical data to inform academic research (see British Academy, 2012; Higher Education Funding Council for England [HEFCE], 2005; Lynch et al., 2007; MacInnes, 2010; McVie, Coxon, Hawkins, Palmer, & Rice, 2008; Parker, Dobson, Scott, Wyman, & Landén, 2008; Rendall, 2003; Williams, Collett, & Rice, 2004). This decline has a multitude of reasons, including:

- a 'cultural shift' towards qualitative approaches since the 1960s and a privileging of theorising over empirical analysis (Blane, 2003; Parker et al., 2008);
- ongoing student dissatisfaction with what they perceive to be a 'difficult' subject (Williams, Payne, Hodgkinson, & Poade, 2008);
- the marketisation of UK universities, since the last 1990s and its incumbent focus on student 'experience' (Scott Jones & Goldring, 2014);
- declining levels of numeracy skills and rising 'maths anxiety' (Scott Jones & Goldring, 2014; Vorderman, Budd, Dunne, Hart, & Porkess, 2011).

This mixture of disciplinary fashion shifts, the emergence of the student as 'consumer' and the long-standing British 'problem' with number, impacts on the educational life course of the typical Sociology student. At A-level, which is the main introduction to the discipline for the majority of British undergraduates,[1] methods work is light on QM and mark schemes are designed in such a way that avoiding the QM questions has little overall impact on final grades (Scott Jones & Goldring, 2014). Thus on entry to university, most Sociology students do not expect to do statistical analysis as part of their degree (Williams et al., 2004, 2008) and perceive it as a marginal subject at best. Most QM is delivered within compulsory research methods modules, often jostling for space alongside qualitative methods (MacInnes, 2010) and low level QM skills predominate (Scott Jones & Goldring, 2014; Williams et al., 2008). Few degree programmes offer specialist options in QM (MacInnes, 2010; Scott Jones & Goldring, 2014; Williams et al., 2008). It is hardly surprising then that so few pursue QM at postgraduate level, with only 21% of ESRC funded projects being solely QM in approach (Economic and Social Research Council, Heads and Professors of Sociology, British Sociological Association, 2010). Consequently, the number of QM-skilled academics is low and there is a dearth of published outputs that have a QM focus; Payne, Williams, and Chamberlain (2004) reviewed the QM element in empirical articles published in the four main Sociology journals between 1999 and 2000; only 14.3% (35 of 244) of articles were quantitative and the majority (40.6%) were qualitative. Additionally, 37.7% were non-empirical and 7.4% were mixed methods. The type of QM approaches within these articles was basic, with most being univariate analysis. The *International Benchmarking Review of Sociology* (Economic and Social Research Council, Heads and Professors of Sociology, British Sociological Association, 2010) also looked at journal articles (specifically the 2008 *British Journal of Sociology*) and found that 47% of articles had a QM focus. However, of the 47% of QM articles in the *British Journal of Sociology*, only half of the first-named authors were British. Much of the reporting of the decline of QM within UK social science has focussed on curricula and research outputs.

However, one group remain the key to the future health (and growth) of QM in the UK: teachers, in both the university and secondary school sectors.[2] Such teachers will train, inspire, enthuse and encourage the next generation of QM specialists working in the UK labour market and/or academia. No amount of curriculum innovation, specialist teaching technology, and bespoke resources will solve the QM problem without effective teachers of QM.

Background – Where have all the QM teachers gone?

Sociology, in line with many other social sciences, has an ageing profile with 42% of staff aged fifty or over (British Sociological Association [BSA], 2013a; Economic and Social Research Council, Heads and Professors of Sociology, British Sociological Association, 2010; Mills et al., 2006). If we consider the decline in QM within UK social science since the 1960s, we can see the consequences of this demographic shift; the majority of QM active researchers in the UK are over fifty and a steady throughput of doctoral students is not replacing them. MacInnes (2010) estimated that around 10% of UK academics are QM specialists, who are most likely to be in senior positions and less likely to teach. According to MacInnes (2010), the UK's teaching base for QM is small and 'fragile' with around one to three QM specialists per

Department, who may or may not do any teaching. Consequently, most staff teaching QM are not specialists and have low levels of QM skills (MacInnes, 2010; Williams et al., 2004, 2008). Typically, staff perceive QM teaching to be 'difficult', partly due to their own low level of skills and partly due to student attitudes to the subject; thus the teaching is often passed on to new or junior staff (McVie et al., 2008; Williams et al., 2004). This creates a 'circle of underachievement' whereby Sociology undergraduates exposed to low levels of QM may not be taught well, often by staff with anti-QM attitudes (Gibbs, 2010). This leads them to shun the subject at postgraduate level, which in turn leads to a further decline in the subject. They may also be poor teachers of QM who communicate negativity about QM leading the students to disengage, further reinforcing poor teaching and on the cycle goes.

Vorderman et al. (2011) describes a similar 'circle of underachievement' in relation to the teaching of maths (another 'difficult' subject, with an image problem) across the educational life course from early years to secondary school. Clearly, a key lever in challenging student attitudes to QM, and encouraging them to pursue the subject post-graduation, is effective teaching by competent (in skills and knowledge) and confident teachers.

Waiting for the culture shift; the importance of upskilling

In response to the issues outlined, the ESRC, in conjunction with the British Academy, funded two programmes in 2011 consisting of twenty projects (each three years long) targeting QM at undergraduate level. One focused on curriculum innovation (ESRC CI stream) and the other on staff training (ESRC RDI stream). These projects are ending and their impact and outputs are only now emerging and being disseminated. Building on this funding is the creation in 2013 of the 15 Q-Step Centres funded by the Nuffield Foundation, the ESRC and HEFCE to address QM decline and encourage a throughput of QM-literate graduates and postgraduates. Other QM initiatives complement these large-scale funding initiatives, such as the Royal Statistical Society's 'Getstats' campaign and the British British Academy's (2012) 'Society Counts' position paper.

However, as ambitious and potentially culture changing these projects may be, they are long-term in scale; we may not see the shift for at least ten years. In addition, predicated on this model is the belief that these initiatives will disseminate good practice across the sector. There remains an immediate need to 'plug' the skills gap of those staff whose job it is to teach the current cohort of students with QM; therefore, the upskilling of staff is a vital interim strategy to deliver effective QM teaching. The upskilling of staff was a strategy adopted by several of the ESRC RDI projects, and this paper focuses on one specific project[3] that centred on the Department of Sociology at Manchester Metropolitan University (henceforth MMU).

Context – the department as a microcosm of QM in the UK

The Department of Sociology at MMU represents a microcosm of all the issues relating to the UK's 'quants problem' as outlined previously. It is one of the largest departments of Sociology in the UK (with almost 800 students across three years of study). In the academic year 2011–2012, prior to the ESRC RDI grant award, the Department taught QM to undergraduates via two compulsory research methods unit ('Understanding Social Research') and 'Practice of Social Enquiry', which later (in 2012) became 'Becoming a Social Researcher'. The former was a year one module, the latter, a year two module. Both modules had a split between qualitative and quantitative approaches; the former always in the first term to avoid, 'scaring the students' as one staff member put it. The year one module dedicated only a third of curriculum space to QM, specifically basic descriptive statistics, whereas in year two QM comprised fifty percent of the curriculum. In year two students studied secondary data analysis of a large national data-set via SPSS up to simple multivariate analysis using a control variable and the Elaboration Model. The one-hour lecture followed by an SPSS lab session was the mode of delivery for both modules. There were no QM specialists in either teaching team; indeed staff allocated to teach on the methods team self-identified as a coalition of 'the new, crazy, and unwilling'. They consisted of new staff ('the new') given no choice what to teach, graduate teaching assistants in it 'for the money' ('the unwilling'), and a small group of staff who actually wanted to teach QM ('the crazy'). A focus group of QM teachers, run by the project team, indicated that they felt 'side-lined' and 'unloved' within the Department. Williams et al. (2004) and MacInnes (2010) found similar attitudes among QM teachers.

The year one module had the lowest attendance (approximately 35–40% attending weekly classes on a regular basis) and highest fail rate (30% in 2011–2012) of any year one module; the year two module had extremely low attendance and the highest fail rate (25% in 2011–2012) of any module run within the Department. The second year module had the lowest average coursework mark (55% in 2011–2012) and both modules had very poor student ratings (3.3 out of 5) in the termly student module surveys. The student survey data for both modules identified 'poor teaching' and 'low levels of support' as central issues; students described QM particularly as 'boring', 'difficult' and 'irrelevant'. Only a handful of students did quantitative dissertations; an advanced QM third year option had not run for many years owing, in part, to a lack of specialist staff. The increasing scrutiny by the university of key indicators of student experience, such as satisfaction survey scores, progression rates, and mark ranges, led to pressure on the module teams. This pressure was evident at a programme review meeting, when it was suggested that QM be removed from the compulsory methods modules and be made optional, condemned to disappear via the discourse of 'student choice'. Fortunately, key members of the research methods team resisted this move, but clearly the existing QM provision needed reform.

The project team conducted an anonymous web-based survey of all Department teaching staff in May 2011 to review quantitative skills. Only four of 37 staff self-identified as quantitative researchers. The remaining research active staff were overwhelmingly qualitative in focus and several were 'anti-method'. Ironically, none of the quantitative researchers currently taught on a research methods module, although all had taught research methods (including quantitative) in the past. The survey revealed that 18 staff members had been involved in teaching QM to undergraduates during their careers. The majority of staff who had taught QM had only received introductory level training, usually while doing postgraduate study. Yet, of these 18, around half admitted to not feeling 'confident' in teaching QM, including SPSS. Around half the Department's staff expressed an interest in developing their skills, primarily for teaching purposes, but a third also keen to develop their skills to use in their personal academic research. Those staff who had received staff development in QM from the university's learning and teaching programme expressed dissatisfaction with a course designed and delivered by and for physical scientists. As one respondent stated, 'it was all pointy clicky, numbers stuff and I was baffled'. This was the context to the ESRC RDI bid: how do we upskill non-QM specialists to make them competent and confident teachers and through this, ultimately enhance the student's learning of QM?

Initial plan – no more pointy clicky, numbers stuff

The initial plan was to establish two staff training courses, which all staff teaching QM would have to attend. The first module ('Introduction to Secondary Data Analysis' [ISDA]) would cover all the QM content currently found in the curriculum and a second module ('Advanced Secondary Data Analysis' [ASDA]) that would follow on and enable staff to revive the mothballed third year QM option and perhaps conduct their own QM research. ISDA would run on a termly basis; it would be student-centred and aimed to 'demystify' quantitative analysis for what were overwhelmingly qualitative researchers, starting first with a focus on core numbers-work. The plan was to create a peer-support system to offer help outside of class time, alongside termly 'teaching QM' workshops to share good practice, talk, 'vent' and generally create a collective sensibility.

In January 2012, ISDA was launched and all staff teaching QM were told to attend. It was due to run as a 10-week, two-hour, lab based workshop, with a final assessment. However, attendance at the weekly lab sessions soon dwindled and those that did attend began to sound like their students, failing to see the relevance of what they were doing, struggling with the statistics ('I'm rubbish at maths'), and generally becoming frustrated with 'pointy clicky' SPSS. The peer support system struggled too, as staff disengaged from the course and later revealed (via follow-up focus groups) that they felt 'embarrassed' to reveal their struggles. At the end of the first run of ISDA, the project team reflected on the experience and staff feedback and realised that the initial approach had mirrored all the mistakes and flawed assumptions made when delivering QM to students:

- Making something compulsory does not necessarily guarantee engagement nor does it mean individuals will see its relevance. There has to be a system of incentives in place to encourage engagement.
- Technical proficiency with SPSS, or other software, does not equate to QM competence. Learning to navigate SPSS and producing outputs is low skill and can be done with little competence with statistics.
- Conceptual understanding of material does not bring with it confidence to teach. To teach confidently, teachers need pedagogic frameworks upon which to place their conceptual knowledge.
- Not all learning is linear and progressive. Individuals learn at different paces and in different ways; sometimes repetition and reinforcement occur before learning moves forward.
- We should not presume that academics have strong numeracy skills or confidence with number. Sociologists, for example, are more likely to share the same low level of maths qualifications as their students and are more likely to have studied social science or humanities A-levels, which are typically 'numbers-lite'.
- That a grasp of the 'basics' will lead inexorably on to interest in and progress with more advanced skills. Individuals need to identify the value in advancing skills that they find challenging.

Through reflection, the project team realised that the goal of the project, the acquiring of specific knowledge by the staff, had led to the needs of the 'students' (the non-QM literate staff) being subsumed by the needs of the 'tutors' (the project staff). The project staff designed the module with their needs at the heart of the curriculum and not the staff-learners, that is, with the view of 'this is what we need to cover' rather than 'how do we cover' and that was a fatal mistake. It is also a common mistake in the design of university curricula, which typically follow a linear model built on the presumption of incremental learning; the tutor designs a module where each week builds on the next and presumes that the students are building their knowledge each week in delineated blocks and can see the connections between material. However, this model is tutor driven, not student centred and the project team realised that although linearity and incremental progression were desirable, this was not realistic. The project team conflated competence with confidence, but confidence is key to effective teaching. Even those staff-learners who completed ISDA did not feel any higher levels of confidence, despite agreeing that they had improved their understanding of QM concepts and SPSS. The project team tore up the ISDA programme and a new model was developed.

Technical conceptual pedagogic practical – a soothing holistic approach

Central to the project team's endeavour was the need to create a holistic approach to upskilling that was would be sensitive to staff needs, but that had pedagogy (and the student) at its centre. Influenced by Freire's (1996) theory of conscientisation we sought to decentralise the power dynamic of the learning process by starting at the level of the needs of learners and what would critically empower them to become active consumers and producers of knowledge. The decentring of classroom power allows learners to develop a critical consciousness of not only themselves as learners, i.e. what academic baggage/preconceptions/blockages, they bring to a setting but additionally it challenges the hierarchy of the classroom, i.e. that teacher knows best. This approach is both liberating for teachers but potentially more challenging. This process of decentralisation was the product of the project team's reflection of their own practices (and presumptions) and evaluation of the staff responses to the first run of ISDA. The result was the Technical-Conceptual-Pedagogic-Practical (TCP) approach as shown in Figure 1, whereby the project team identified the four key elements that they needed to embed within the course if they were to succeed in the creation of confident, as well as competent, teachers.

Technical – How do I?

The module had to allow the staff to learn to use the SPSS software, with confidence, but not in such a way that they reverted to the 'pointy clicky' approach of instrumental button pushing, without understanding the concepts or theory behind the output tables. The staff-learners had identified SPSS as a barrier to their learning; they found the software user 'unfriendly' and much valuable lab time was taken with explaining how to work SPSS, as opposed to interpreting SPSS outputs. Additionally, staff themselves wanted a user-friendly SPSS manual for their own teaching in the lab. A student workbook was produced which covered each key SPSS skill needed, along with worked examples, review questions, and activities to do on a practice data-set. The workbook activities were incremental, they began with the easiest (opening SPSS) to

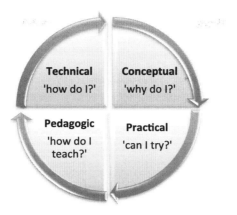

Figure 1. The TCP model.

the hardest (multivariate analysis). The staff-learners could work through the book at their own pace in the labs and return to activities with which they struggled. This was also a resource that they could road test for their own students. The idea was to (following Freire, 1996) empower the student to become an active agent in his or her own learning, using the book as a guide, going at his or her own pace. Thus removing the need for the lab tutor to waste time going over technical issues that are easily learnt and best achieved via self-directed SPSS work.

The lab tutor used the lab's media desk to go through activities together via an 'I do one, we do one, you do one' approach: the tutor demonstrates one task on SPSS, for example, how to interpret a frequency table, using the interactive whiteboard. Then the class do one together, using the interactive whiteboard and review it as a group. Finally, the students do it themselves on their own computers and the tutor monitors their progress by circulating through the lab. This approach created a sense of a collective learning space that helped the group to create a shared identity as learners. This emerging identity helped to make the classroom space 'safe' for staff to learn and crucially make mistakes. Throughout tutors reiterated that learning how to navigate SPSS was the least important of the four elements and that it was important for learners to see it as an instrumental tool for analysis, as opposed to a conceptual framework.

Conceptual – Why do I?

In conjunction with the technical aspects of learning a software package, it was crucial that the staff-learners understood how to apply concepts. The 'pointy clicky' approach often emerges due to a lack of conceptual understanding; individual students struggle with a specific concept and over-focus on generating SPSS outputs without the ability to fully analyse them. Meyer and Land's (2003, 2005) theory of 'threshold concepts' and barriers to learning, informed our approach to the conceptual part of the course. A 'threshold concept' is a concept, or theory, that students must understand in order to move forward in their learning. However, a failure to understand a 'threshold concept' blocks a student's progress and becomes a barrier to learning; Figure 2 illustrates the issue:

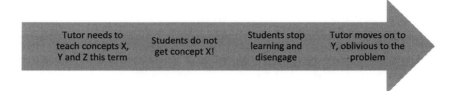

Figure 2. Barriers to learning.

'Threshold concepts' may vary by cohort or class and may emerge at any time on a module; therefore the identification of 'threshold concepts' is crucial both for the design of a course and for its delivery. Quantitative methods have been identified as having a great many challenging concepts (Williams et al., 2008), often ones that are not used commonly outside of the subject due to the marginalisation of QM (MacInnes, 2010). For example, numbers themselves were the first threshold that the majority of our students had to breach; 'maths anxiety' as a barrier to learning has been well documented (e.g. Onwuegbuzie & Wilson, 2003). We addressed this through a numeracy diagnostic at the start of the module to assess the cohort's numeracy levels. The findings from the diagnostic were used to create online numeracy support resources and allowed teaching staff to build-in extra support sessions on specific skills, for example, decimal points and percentages. Additionally, 'maths anxiety' was addressed by stressing that the numbers were 'telling stories', thus we appealed to the students' pre-existing narrative and critical skills. All this was actively facilitated by the constant message that quantitative analysis is 'not maths'. The identification of 'threshold concepts' is an ongoing process that requires teaching staff to gauge constantly student progress, thus concept testing becomes invaluable. A virtual learning environment (specifically Moodle) was used to deliver quizzes and self-tests, so that tutors could see which concepts staff-learners were struggling with and address the gaps in learning, with either extra practice or a review of the concept.

This approach means that the course must be sufficiently flexible that some sessions may be repeated or later ones removed to accommodate areas that were missed. Allowing students to learn at their own pace meant that we needed to provide additional 'pop up labs' where they could catch up with materials missed. However, it is crucial that the tutor goes at the right pace for the class throughout. The project team incorporated this flexible approach and found that the staff-learners progressed quickly through some elements of the curriculum and needed longer for others. This meant much shuffling of sessions and review of material, but the flexibility resulted in less anxiety for the learners and allowed them to feel valued; their learning needs were prioritised over time or curriculum demands.

Pedagogic – How do I teach?

Central to the new approach was to embed pedagogy within each session. The staff-learners frequently voiced the concern that 'I get this ... but how the hell do I teach it?' or 'don't ask me to teach this!' Therefore each session combined SPSS tasks, and concept learning, alongside informal discussions on different ways to deliver material, whether in lecture or in a lab setting. The tutors would lead this with examples from their own practice and then the group would evaluate, critique, and offer additional ideas. One central element of this was reflective practice; staff-learners were encouraged to reflect on their own anxieties, troubles and difficulties with QM as a means to appreciate better how their own students may feel. One example of this was their own lack of confidence with numbers and anxiety towards them; the appreciation that their own students may be feeling as they do was both liberating and empowering. This approach drew on Vygotsky's (1978) idea that learning does not happen in isolation; the classroom is not hermetically sealed off from the outside world, rather learners and learning exists outside of the classroom and learners bring baggage into it. Reflection can be a means to empower the learner and make them an active participant within their learning. As this happened among peers, it allowed the staff-learners group to form an identity as learners, with a shared experience. The project team facilitated these discussions and the group agreed a shared code of 'what is discussed in lab stays in lab'; it was deemed a confidential learning space where issues could be explored without other staff members, external to the group, finding out.

Additionally, the staff-learners were encouraged to reflect on how they and others learn; preconceptions were challenged. For example, typically students are seen as a uniform group who all learn in the same way at the same pace. However, students enter university with at least thirteen years of educational 'baggage', including, bad (and good) study habits, anxieties, and specific learning styles (often laid down early in childhood). The staff-learners were encouraged to reflect on their own learning styles (and 'baggage') as a means to explore their students' perspectives. The importance of a diversity in modes of delivery of material in order to address different learning styles was explored as was the importance of not viewing all learning as linear. Teachers and curricula need to be flexible. This exploration of learning styles led to innovation in practice, including, how to incorporate kinaesthetic and visual learning into lectures. This dialogic element also challenged the staff's earlier identification of the lab sessions as boring, lacking interactivity and being 'sterile' in contrast to their regular teaching spaces, which were designed for dialogue.

Various pedagogic techniques were introduced to the sessions to facilitate learning, but also to demonstrate how the staff-learners might support and deliver material to their students. Various scaffolding techniques (Wood, Bruner, & Ross, 1976; Wood & Wood, 1996) were utilised, such as concept testing, and one popular one was the 'pink cards'; these were (pink) task cards that listed a set number of formative tasks that the tutors could use to map and assess progress and learning. The tasks were completed at the staff-learners' pace enabling them to be agents of their own learning. The 'pink cards' also allowed the tutor to monitor progress amongst the lab group. This technique proved popular with the staff-learners and subsequently with their students. Staff were encouraged to use classroom technology to facilitate interactivity, including Kahoot[4] quizzes, Socrative discussions, and interactive online data. Staff shared information on resources that they found outside of class.

Practical – Can I have a go?

The final element of this model was a 'learn by doing' approach; the weekly lab tasks, quizzes etc. allowed the staff-learners to 'have a go' at the material. The practical element gave the staff practice time to concretise their learning and to make mistakes; often the most useful insights came from errors. Particularly useful was the assessment exercise, whereby all the staff had to do the assessment that they expected their students to do. This allowed staff to appreciate better their assessment task and mark scheme, leading to much revision of the assessment to make it more user-friendly. This activity made staff much more reflective of how they marked the assessment.

This new model was adopted to coincide with the revamp of the QM curriculum and staff attending the subsequent ISDA modules liked the linkage between actual course content ('this is what I will teach') and the training course. Subsequent sessions (Jan 2013, Sept 2013, and Sept 2014) were better attended and the staff-learners were happier and more comfortable. Staff-learners were encouraged to re-attend sessions on material that they found difficult and this flexible approach was useful as staff-learners used repeat sessions to 'fine tune' on certain topics. This approach led to a greater sense of shared identity and cohesion among the QM team, which greatly facilitated the process of curriculum revision and innovation.

Going further?

The original plan has been to launch an advanced QM training course for staff that would follow on from ISDA. However, it became clear that the timeframe for this was over-ambitious, as it took the staff-learners longer to feel confident with the basics, many retaking specific sessions. A small group of staff-learners were encouraged to attend external advanced training courses, but were disaffected with these due to their lack of consideration for pedagogy either in their delivery or content. By summer 2014, an advanced module was delivered in-house to the original ISDA cohort and this will be repeated in summer 2015.

Valuing QM/valuing staff

Upskilling staff does not just mean putting them on a training course, nor does it mean giving them bespoke materials to teach. Rather it demands the creation of a culture that values both QM and the staff delivering it (MacInnes, 2010; Williams et al., 2004). The project team's realisation that staff would not engage with the training just because 'they have to' was important. Ely and Ely (1995, p. 25) highlights that lecturers 'need to know that time and energy invested in acquiring new skills will be recognised and rewarded by their employer'. The project team then had to confront the question of what would incentivise the staff.

Qualifications?

In the UK, it is not a statutory requirement that university teachers have a teaching qualification or engage in continuous professional development, although the reports by Dearing (1997) and Browne (2010) recommended both. The foundation of the Higher Education Academy in 2003 and the more recent UK Professional Standards Framework in 2011, have aided the professionalisation (and its accreditation) of university teaching. Nevertheless, the onus remains on the individual university to prioritise training. Yet Guskey (2000) has emphasised the fact that improvements within education rarely occur without a process of professional development. The project team were committed to getting the two staff QM training courses accredited by the university, so staff could use the course to gain credits towards a PGCAcPrac or MA in Academic Practice. Two problems quickly emerged; the first was the difficult and slow internal accreditation process and the second was the fact that most of the staff had a PGCAcPrac already and had no interest in gaining further credits or qualifications. The pursuit of accreditation was abandoned early on. However, by the final year (2014) of the project the university had streamlined its approach to staff training via a new flexible CPD system whereby diverse forms of training could be rewarded via a points system. Therefore, ISDA and ASDA are now accredited within the university's CPD framework. Additionally, the university is currently rolling-out CPD as a means to prioritise and normalise staff training.

Workload recognition?

The biggest driver of staff engagement was the decision to allocate additional workload recognition to those staff doing the training and teaching on the QM modules. The Department's workload model allowed the project team to do this and fortunately, the Head of Department was willing to divert extra resources. The pre-project complaint of 'not having enough time' to either teach QM or train in QM was addressed. The workload support was important because it showed that the Department valued the QM staff; a group who had once felt marginalised. This workload approach also resulted in other staff wanting to take the training and shift into methods teaching, thus increasing the QM pool of talent.

Valuing QM

It was important for the Departmental culture to value QM. Therefore, the project team worked with the Head of Department to change the Departmental culture. The Departmental strategic plan (2013) identified QM as one of its priorities, both for teaching and research. Teaching technology in labs and lecture theatres was funded to facilitate interactivity. In addition, pressure was exerted on the wider faculty administration to refit all the teaching labs, equipping them with new computers and interactive media desks. As well as staff receiving additional workload, all QM classes were given additional contact teaching hours; three hours per module, per week, in contrast to the two hours per week of a non-QM module. This change in Departmental culture not only valued QM staff, but also signalled to other staff the value of QM and its place within the Department. One outcome of this shift and of the training course has been the embedding of statistical and data literacy within non-methods modules, which started in 2013–2014. As other staff see the value of QM (and its potential value to them too) it has been easier for the QM staff to run an embedding programme. Those staff that participate in embedding also receive workload relief to train in QM and to teach embedded material. This in turn strengthens the Department's QM culture through the normalisation of QM within the wider curriculum and staff.

Without the wider Departmental recognition it would have been difficult for the project to have made the impact that it had; workload was an essential driver, as staff are busy and have many demands on their time. A less sympathetic Head of Department, or the absence of a clear workload model, would have made the training course and teaching QM less attractive. In the Department, as is common in most Sociology departments, the QM staff are the minority; therefore, the worldview of the majority of staff is often to view QM as marginal to the curriculum. The allocation of new or junior staff to the QM teaching teams can reinforce this view. If the departmental culture changes to value QM, via resourcing, infrastructural change, strategic prioritisation etc. then all staff can see the potential worth in QM. Such a departmental shift in staff worldviews has an important impact on students' attitudes to QM too. Staff are crucial in shaping students' attitudes to QM (Williams et al., 2008); one barrier to learning QM is student attitudes, even if QM teachers are fantastic they may fail to shift student perceptions if all their other tutors and modules are non-QM or even anti-QM. Thus is it important that departmental culture identifies QM as an essential element and that normalises QM via embedding (and training).

Impact – confident staff/confident students

As the project nears its end, the impacts have been overwhelmingly positive for staff and students.

Staff

All staff who now teach QM have been on the basic training course, including graduate teaching assistants. A small number have done the advanced training and more will take this later in this academic year (2014–2015). The QM staff are now a strong team who have expanded, following new appointments that prioritised QM, and who regularly share good practice. One outcome of the training course is a shift towards team teaching, with staff co-delivering lectures and even labs. This provides for a more dynamic delivery but also affords informal peer review and support, which further informs practice. Student free text comments in termly module satisfaction surveys have noted, 'The way the team work together to cover each other, they are very passionate'; 'Lectures this year have become much more active and interesting'; 'The enthusiasm of the tutors and lecturers. It's a really dry subject, made much better by the quality of the staff'. An interesting outcome of our approach was that in the past getting tutors to work on the QM modules was challenging while now we are in a position where we have more colleagues wanting to teach than we have available classes. The strong group identity and culture of shared practice has led to the QM staff taking a lead in Departmental learning and teaching initiatives, including demonstrating how to use technology to enhance interactivity, the role of concept testing, and the importance of addressing the student as an individual learner. Staff have shifted from self-identifying as 'not a quants person' to 'I'm on the quants team'.

Students

The two large compulsory methods modules in years one and two have been revised in the light of this training course. The specific curriculum is similar; indeed the QM is now at a slightly higher level and there is more of it (50% of the curriculum) in the first year. However, the style of delivery in both lab and lecture is radically different, drawing on the pedagogic theories that underpin the training course; what worked for the teachers now works for the students. Concept testing, diagnostic maths testing, practical examples, formative assessment via the 'pink task cards', an SPSS workbook, interactive technology, and a range of delivery styles (including visual and kinaesthetic) place the onus on the student as an active participant in his or her own learning (following Meyer & Land, 2003; Vygotsky, 1978). The students are more competent and confident; the second year QM module has one of the highest pass rates (95% in 2013–2014), average coursework marks (65% in 2013–2014), and student satisfaction scores (4.3 out of a possible five, in 2013–2014) in the Department. The first year module is not far behind in terms of results, student progression and satisfaction. Final year students even asked for a third year QM option at the end of the last academic year (2013–2014) and 38% (32 out of 85) are doing QM dissertations in the current academic year (2014–2015) compared with only 2% (2 out of 121) doing QM dissertations in 2013–2014. The number taking dissertations is partly due to the creation of placement based QM dissertations, but if the Department had not upskilled their staff then the placement programme would not have worked as there would have been insufficient staff to support it.

Final comments

Since this project started in late 2011, the position of QM and its value within the Department has changed radically. This project enabled the Department to upskill staff, but additionally to revamp curricula, placing the student and pedagogy at its heart. Within the context of the Department of Sociology at MMU, the upskilling of staff is continuing, and is valued and rewarded in a range of ways. Some of those upskilled staff are now using QM within their research and staff who do not teach on the methods modules now want to take the training, as they want to embed QM and are interested in conducting QM research. The project team are now making the QM training available to staff outside the Department both within the university and for external organisations.

Lessons from the experience described in this paper include that universities need to take the training of staff more seriously. Often a 'deficit' model is applied whereby staff attend courses because they are deemed to 'lack' skills rather than because they may wish to develop skills and new competencies. Thus, training is identified with a 'problem' as opposed to an enhancement. Ironically, university teachers perceive themselves as able to teach through their acquisition of specialist research knowledge, with scant reflection on the art or practice of teaching. Until universities reward good teaching as they reward good research, this will not change. On a more positive note, the rise of the student as consumer and the switch towards an emphasis on the student experience and satisfaction is leading to an increased focus on teaching quality and practice. Continuing professional development should be a key component of all university teachers and be rewarded within university pay and progression schemes. One positive outcome of the QM 'problem' in the UK has been the emergence of a strong QM teachers' community who share practice and opinion. The ESRC's CI and RDI projects are producing a range of outputs and resources, which are now coming on stream to support QM teachers. Additionally, the issue of statistical literacy and the strategic importance of QM has resulted in a myriad of resources to support teachers and value QM for teachers and students alike, for example the QM Initiative (Economic & Social Research Council [ESRC], 2013). The creation of the Q-Step Centres will add to this growing body of teaching resources and models. The challenge lies in ensuring that QM teachers outside of this network are supported via resources and networking opportunities. One final positive reflection would be that those who teach QM have much to teach those staff who are faced with the problems of other 'difficult to teach' subjects, such as social theory. Many of the pedagogic strategies that we have found effective in delivering QM could (and should) be used as exemplars of good practice for all challenging subject areas.

Disclosure statement

No potential conflict of interest were reported by the authors.

Funding

This work was supported by the Economic and Social Research Council [grant number ES/J011703/1].

Notes

1. 80% of British students studying for a degree in Sociology studied the subject at A2 level (British Sociological Association [BSA], 2013b).
2. See a discussion of some of the key factors affecting secondary school teachers' ability to deliver QM within A level curricula in Scott Jones and Goldring (2014).
3. ESRC 'No More Point Clicky, numbers stuff; building staff quantitative skills', ES/J011703/1.
4. Kahoot and Socrative are classroom response systems that utilise game-based blended learning including polls, quizzes, debates and so forth. Both systems allow learners to interact within the classroom via the use of mobile devices. Such technologies are particularly effective in engaging all learners and allowing tutors to receive instant feedback to class material.

References

Blane, D. (2003). The use of quantitative medical sociology. *Sociology of Health and Illness, 25*, 115–130.
British Academy. (2012). *Society counts*. London: Author.
British Sociological Association. (2013a). *Mapping sociology project report*. Durham: Author.
British Sociological Association. (2013b). *Discovering sociology*. Durham: British Sociological Association.
Browne, J. (2010). *Securing a sustainable future for higher education*. Report of the independent review of higher education funding and student finance. London: Department for Business, Innovation and Skills.

Dearing, R. (1997). *Higher education in the learning society*. Report of the national committee of enquiry into higher education. London: HMSO.
Economic and Social Research Council (2013). *ESRC/HEA QM initiative website* [online]. Retrieved October 8, 2013, from http://www.quantitativemethods.ac.uk/
Economic and Social Research Council, Heads and Professors of Sociology, British Sociological Association. (2010) *International benchmarking review of sociology* [online]. Retrieved October 10, 2012, from http://www.esrc.ac.uk/_images/Int_benchmarking_sociology_tcm8-4556.pdf
Ely, P., & Ely, A. (1995). IT training and staff development in universities. *Education and Training, 37*, 18–30.
Freire, P. (1996). *Pedagogy of the oppressed*. London: Penguin.
Gibbs, G. R. (2010). Mathematics and statistics in the social sciences. In C. M. Marr & M. J. Grove (Eds.), *Responding to the Mathematics problem: The implementation of institutional support mechanisms* (pp. 44–50). St Andrews: The Maths, Stats and OR Network.
Guskey, T. R. (2000). *Evaluating professional development*. London: Sage.
Higher Education Funding Council for England. (2005). *Strategically important and vulnerable subjects; final report of the advisory group* [online]. London: Author. Retrieved December 21, 2012, from http://www.hefce.ac.uk/pubs/hefce/2005/05_24/05_24.pdf
Lynch, R., Maio, G., Moore, G., Moore, L., Orford, S., Robinson, A., … Whitfield, K. (2007). *ESRC/HEFCW scoping study into quantitative methods capacity building in Wales*. Final report to the ESRC and HEFCW [online]. Swindon: ESRC. Retrieved February 25, 2014, from http://www.esrc.ac.uk/_images/Scoping_Study_into_Quantitative_Capacity_Building_in_Wales_tcm8-2724.pdf
MacInnes, J. (2010). *Proposals to support and improve the teaching of quantitative research methods at undergraduate level in the UK* [online]. Swindon: ESRC. Retrieved December 21, 2012, from http://www.esrc.ac.uk/_images/Undergraduate_quantitative_research_methods_tcm8-2722.pdf
McVie, S., Coxon, A., Hawkins, P., Palmer, J., & Rice, R. (2008). *ESRC/SFC scoping study into quantitative methods capacity building in Scotland*. Final Report [online]. Retrieved November 9, 2012, from http://www.esrc.ac.uk/_images/Scoping_Study_into_Quantitative_Capacity_Building_in_Scotland_tcm8-2683.pdf
Meyer, J. H. F., & Land, R. (2003). Threshold concepts and troublesome knowledge: Linkages to ways of thinking and practising within the disciplines. In C. Rust (Ed.), *Improving student learning: Improving student learning theory and practice-ten years on* (pp. 412–424). Oxford: Oxford Centre for Staff and Learning Development.
Meyer, J. H. F., & Land, R. (2005). Threshold concepts and troublesome knowledge (2): Epistemological considerations and a conceptual framework for teaching and learning. *Higher Education, 49*, 373–388.
Mills, D., Jepson, A., Coxon, T., Easterby-Smith, M. P. V., Hawkins, P., & Spencer, J. (2006). *Demographic review of the UK social sciences* [online]. Swindon: ESRC. Retrieved February 25, 2014, from http://www.esrc.ac.uk/_images/demographic_review_tcm8-13533.pdf
Nuffield Foundation. (2013). *Q-step programme website* [online]. Retrieved November 10, 2013, from http://www.nuffieldfoundation.org/q-step
Onwuegbuzie, A. J., & Wilson, V. A. (2003). Statistics anxiety: Nature, etiology, antecedents, effects, and treatments – A comprehensive review of the literature. *Teaching in Higher Education, 8*, 195–209.
Parker, J., Dobson, A., Scott, S., Wyman, M., & Landén, A. S. (2008). *International benchmarking review of best practice in the provision of undergraduate teaching in quantitative methods in the social sciences* [online]. Retrieved October 10, 2012, from http://www.esrc.ac.uk/_images/International_benchmarking_undergraduate_quantitative_methods_tcm8-2725.pdf
Payne, G., Williams, M., & Chamberlain, S. (2004). Methodological pluralism in British sociology. *Sociology, 38*, 153–163.
Rendall, M. (2003). *Quantitative research: A scoping study for the learning and skills research centre* [online]. Retrieved December 21, 2012, from http://www.tlrp.org/rcbn/capacity/Activities/Themes/Secondary/lsda_quant_research.pdf

Scott Jones, J., & Goldring, J. E. (2014). *Skills in mathematics and statistics in sociology and tackling transition. Higher education academy STEM project: Skills in mathematics and statistics in the disciplines and tackling transition.* York: HEA.

Vorderman, C., Budd, C., Dunne, R., Hart, M. & Porkess, R. (2011). *A world class mathematics education for all our young people* [online]. Retrieved November 11, 2012, from http://www.tsm-resources.com/pdf/VordermanMathsReport.pdf

Vygotsky, L. S. (1978). *Mind in society: Development of higher psychological processes.* Boston, MA: Harvard University Press.

Williams, M., Collett, C., & Rice, R. (2004). *Baseline study of quantitative methods in British sociology.* Birmingham/Durham: C-SAP/BSA.

Williams, M., Payne, G., Hodgkinson, L., & Poade, D. (2008). Does British sociology count? Sociology students' attitudes toward quantitative methods. *Sociology, 42*, 1003–1021.

Wood, D. J., Bruner, J. S., & Ross, G. (1976). The role of tutoring in problem solving. *Journal of Child Psychology and Psychiatry, 17*, 89–100.

Wood, D., & Wood, H. (1996). Vygotsky, tutoring and learning. *Oxford Review of Education, 22*, 5–16.

Embedding quantitative skills into the social science curriculum: case studies from Manchester

Jennifer Buckley, Mark Brown, Stephanie Thomson, Wendy Olsen and Jackie Carter

Social Statistics, University of Manchester, Humanities Bridgeford Street, Manchester, UK

> Those aiming to respond to the recognised shortage in quantitative skills within the UK social sciences have increasingly focused on the content of undergraduate degree programmes. Problems occur when quantitative methods are generally confined to a dedicated module, detached from substantive topics. This model makes it hard for students to understand or engage with the contribution of quantitative research to their discipline and can perpetuate negative perceptions of quantitative training. We suggest a solution to this problem is 'quantitative embedding', in which quantitative evidence and methods are incorporated into substantive teaching in the social sciences. We illustrate quantitative embedding with case studies from an ESRC funded project based in The University of Manchester, where teaching partnerships have developed curriculum innovations in Sociology and Politics. The paper then discusses the challenges of disseminating quantitative embedding, highlighting the need to bridge separate communities of practice that can isolate quantitative specialists.

In recognising a shortage of quantitative skills in the UK Social Science community, scholars have highlighted shortcomings in the way quantitative methods (QM) are taught in undergraduate programmes (Falkingham & McGowan, 2011; MacInnes, 2009; Parker, Dobson, Scott, Wyman, & Landén, 2008). These reports observe that while on most programmes some quantitative training is now compulsory, for many students it is something detached from the rest of their degree, lacking relevance to the major disciplinary themes covered in their substantive courses. This observation may highlight a problem with the methods courses themselves, which tend to teach the mechanics of data analysis. Equally, it might be because much 'non-methods' teaching lacks quantitative examples and references to the contribution of quantitative approaches to subject knowledge. Against a background of widely reported student anxiety over quantitative data (Adeney & Carey, 2011; Howery & Havidan, 2006; Slootmaeckers, Kerremans, & Adriaensen, 2014; Williams, Payne, Hodgkinson, & Poade, 2008), the marginalisation of quantitative evidence in substantive teaching is a clear obstacle to getting students to see quantitative methods training as anything more than a module to be got through.

In the UK, alienation from quantitative methods among undergraduates may reflect the wider marginalisation of quantitative methods within parts of the social science research community. For example, a content analysis of leading sociology journals in 2004 found that less than 9% of papers with empirical content used quantification (Payne, Williams, & Chamberlin, 2004). Despite major initiatives to increase quantitative training at postgraduate level, Wiles, Durrant, De Broe, and Powell (2009) found that the 'anti-quantitative' attitudes observed among Social Science undergraduates were also evident among doctoral students, with less than a quarter of Sociology and Politics students using any quantitative data in their PhDs. This concerning state of affairs threatens the motivation and ability of a new generation of social scientists to engage with some of the classic texts in UK social science or with quantitatively advanced outputs from the USA.

In response to the quantitative deficit in the undergraduate curriculum, this paper discusses an approach for teaching social science research methods where quantitative data and methods are embedded within the substantive curriculum. In presenting this approach, we are keen to dissociate from any suggestion that quantitative approaches are superior to qualitative methods and traditions (see Byrne, 2012) and reject as unhelpful any framing of the debate as a quantitative vs. qualitative methodological divide. Instead, we emphasise how embedding can help students develop the skills and experiences they need as social scientists to evaluate the usefulness of various methodological approaches. Through examples from an ESRC-funded teaching project based at the University of Manchester, UK, we discuss what quantitative embedding can look like in practice and the collaborative teaching partnerships that have been a key component of our model. We then evaluate our experiences of embedding and review the challenges and opportunities involved in adopting such a model across the Higher Education (HE) community.

The case for quantitative embedding in the substantive curriculum

Our approach developed in response to feedback from students that methods teaching seems divorced from the rest of the curriculum, something to be endured rather than enthused about (MacInnes, 2009; Wathan, Brown, & Williamson, 2011; Williams & Sutton, 2011). Based on the study by Williams et al. (2008), a survey of second year sociology students confirmed there was high anxiety around the use of statistics and a common perception that quantitative research examples are infrequently used in other course units. Low prior mathematics attainment could be a contributory factor. Hodgen, Pepper, and London (2010) confirmed that among the 24 countries studied the UK had the lowest proportion studying maths post age 16. However, we view the failure to establish the relevance of quantitative skills as a greater barrier, echoing others in the field (Adeney & Carey, 2011; Chamberlain, Hillier, & Signoretta, 2014; Williams et al., 2008). This is not to deny the importance of mathematical knowledge in methods teaching but to question whether 'more' school mathematics is likely to make a difference to students' attitudes towards and attainment in research methods.

In teaching research methods, we are asking students to do more than simply perform calculations. We try to teach students to become confident and critical interpreters of data for their methodological competence and literacy. Thus, we aim for students to gain conceptual understanding of methodological issues and not just procedural competence. In essence, we face similar problems to school mathematics teachers: how to engage students and give them a 'relational' rather than 'instrumental' understanding of concepts (Skemp, 1976). One approach is to employ 'connectionist teaching' practices. Connectionist teaching encourages students to actively consider how the idea or concept relates to other ideas and concepts; students are encouraged to evaluate the appropriateness of different techniques (Askew, Brown, Rhodes, Johnson, & Wiliam, 1997). In contrast, 'transmissionist' teaching prioritises the learning of techniques and processes, which can then be applied in a variety of situations. A key difference between these two styles, represented here in their ideal form, is the role of examples in learning. For connectionist teachers, examples play a key role in the learning process as students become aware of the role of context in informing their approach to problem solving. By contrast, for transmissionist teachers, examples provide a valuable opportunity to practise processes that have been learned already.

As Vygotsky (1987) argues, understanding the *relationship* between a specific example and an abstract idea is essential to concept formation. Methods teaching that is independent of substantive teaching asks students to learn and apply abstract, generalised ideas rather than providing opportunities to develop deeper, conceptual understanding through the use of detailed, rich examples. Any conceptual understanding that develops independently of real examples risks being incomplete and can lead students to see concepts, and indeed conceptual thinking, as divorced from their main interests (Vygotsky, 1998). Vygotsky's ideas provide a plausible explanation for what we see in practice with methods courses when students find the content detached from reality and hard to learn.

The 'connectionist' teaching strategies favoured by some mathematics educators may offer a useful way forward. Organisation of the school curriculum into separate, examined subjects makes examples of 'connectionist' teaching in schools rare. However, a key development, Realistic Mathematics Education (RME), has been shown to improve problem-solving skills in pupils and increase their interest and confidence in mathematics.[1] The challenge, then, is how to implement such an approach in HE to ensure examples allow conceptual understanding and more active learning by students. We could reasonably expect methods teachers to develop materials using examples from their own fields, but not across all subject areas. Moreover, compartmentalising methods teaching sends a message to students that the context of a problem is less important than the abstract, generalizable principles that underpin the methods used.

Alongside others we propose building bridges between the teaching of methods and substantive course units including the embedding of some aspects of methods teaching into substantive course units (see also Adeney & Carey, 2011; Falkingham & McGowan, 2011; Hampden-Thompson & Sundaram, 2013; Slootmaeckers et al., 2014). Encouragingly, as embedding has become more widespread, studies are producing evidence that the opportunities to learn using data in particular social science contexts can have a positive effect on student attitudes and attainment. Notably, Slootmaeckers et al. (2014) found that students encountering quantitative methods in substantive courses had reduced anxiety over statistics and greater retention of statistics skills.

We further suggest that embedding allows students to develop what Bloom, Englehart, Furst, Hill, and Krathwohl (1956) terms higher-order thinking skills. Bloom et al. (1956), drawing on Vygotsky, suggest that thinking skills vary in difficulty from lower-order skills needed to learn new terms or facts through to higher-order skills needed to evaluate evidence. Course units dedicated to teaching quantitative methods, as they are usually constructed (Parker et al., 2008), start by giving students the opportunity to acquire skills in, what Bloom et al. (1956) term, the knowledge class of the cognitive domain. Students learn new terminology, processes to follow and perhaps technical skills in statistical software. Eventually, they are expected to analyse data and make statements about the relationships between variables, thus demonstrating skills in the analysis class of the cognitive domain. In an embedded model, the problems that a data analyst faces are explored, not just as technical issues, but as real, substantive challenges that require critical attention.

There is a clear case for embedding aspects of methodological teaching in the substantive curriculum; however, this part of the solution is not straightforward to implement. To be successful, embedding activities must be well-planned so that students are able to draw on appropriate materials and exercises to aid their learning. Badly developed materials and activities may reinforce students' negative perceptions of statistics (Slootmaeckers et al., 2014). In the following three sections, we outline how embedding might work in practice with reference to the model developed within our own institution and particular examples of teaching innovations.

Embedding in practice

Our institutional response to the problem of teaching QM started with the existing methods classes. In particular, the core sociology unit was redesigned to mimic the process of doing social research. In our revised model, students learn how to develop and explore theoretically informed and substantively interesting research questions with real survey data. The producing and interpreting of statistics in the practical classes (primarily using SPSS) is thus underlined by clear substantive research goals. For example, we have used the Health Survey for England to explore gendered aspects of obesity and attitudes towards weight and the British Crime Survey to investigate the social determinants of the fear of crime. As well as offering an engaging way of introducing statistical concepts and techniques, this also fosters a critical approach to data and analysis, as the specific research contexts raise issues such as question design, non-response and coding decisions. The changes resulted in clear improvements in student evaluation and, the previously unpopular course was commended for attaining feedback scores in the top 10% of all undergraduate course units in the Faculty. While this was a clearly positive outcome, a well-designed and received methods course is not sufficient; as Chamberlain et al. (2014) found even when a student group rates their methods training highly, most students remain anxious about leaning statistics and lacking confidence in their numeracy skills.

The second element of our strategy focuses on building links in the other direction by embedding quantitative data and research throughout the degree programme. Similar to the approach of Falkingham and McGowan (2011), a central aspect of our model are collaborations between the project team and lecturers. In our case, the project team comprises experienced methods teachers, a specialist in mathematics education and experts in data support services. The partner lecturers participated voluntarily and are all from Politics and Sociology, social sciences discipline areas identified as having the greatest need in the UK for more QM training (MacInnes, 2009). We recognise that this model of teaching partnerships is rarely found naturally in institutions and must be carefully managed. Wenger's (1999) notion of communities of practice is helpful here because it can help us understand how sub-groups within institutions set their own norms and develop their own ways of working which may differ from other sub-groups. The teaching material is constructed through a collaborative partnership, where the substantive lecturer directs the nature and focus of the embedding intervention. This approach aims to tailor new content to the course's learning aims and objectives. The benefits of such collaborations are mutual. Methods teachers benefit as students begin to encounter quantitative data and concepts regularly in substantive course units where lecturers provide extensive additional resources, including expertise and time that can enrich their teaching.

Table 1 summarises the embedding activities developed through 13 teaching partnerships across two academic years. A common element of the collaborative process was a series of consultations between the project team and course unit convenors. The consultation process followed a distinctive path for each partnership but always focused on identifying aspects of the current curriculum that could be enhanced by the integration of quantitative data and methods. Consultations typically started in April to ensure materials could be developed and integrated into the curriculum for the start of term in September. However, collaborative arrangements varied to accommodate the timescale of each partner and the nature of embedding activities, which sometimes needed to be created in parallel with the teaching. As Table 1 shows, collectively our teaching partnerships drew upon an extensive range of data to develop diverse embedding materials and activities.

Case studies of quantitative embedding

Our examples of quantitative embedding are not intended to constitute a one-size fits all version of 'best practice'. Such a prescriptive notion of 'best practice' is unhelpful in this context. Instead, we must consider variations in student intake and adapt teaching to the the group. A notion of 'best practice' may devalue perfectly successful alternative methods of teaching and stifle innovation. Moreover, it may serve to create a power imbalance in collaborative relationships. Thus, it is possible to learn from the experiences of seasoned practitioners without accepting that there is one, best approach.

Making students 'part of the data-set'

Our first example developed through the collaborative partnership to introduce quantitative data and methods to a large politics course unit, *Introduction to Comparative Politics*. The large cohort contains students at different stages and different degree courses. In this partnership, the consultation established an opportunity to build teaching materials linking with the research of one of the course lecturers. The lecturer had been involved in developing survey questions on attitudes to immigration for the British Social Attitudes (BSA) survey. These questions were added to a simple online survey for completion prior to the lecture and we compiled the student data with data for the British public and graduates from the 2011 BSA survey. This exercise makes students 'part of the dataset' and demonstrates the research process moving through the stages of question design through to data collection and data analysis. The survey instrument, exercise of data collection and the resulting data-set provides

Table 1. Summary of teaching partnerships, embedding activities and data sources.

Course unit (discipline area)	Embedding activity	Main data sources
Year 1 (2012/2013)		
Power and Protest (Sociology)	'Are the young politically disengaged?' Debating the evidence from survey data with added data sourcing activity	British Social Attitudes Survey (BSA); Audit of Political Engagement
Sociology of Personal Life (Sociology)	Tutorial on living alone using survey data on solo living and the characteristics of those living alone	Understanding Society
Introduction to Comparative Politics (Politics)	Lecture and tutorial examining attitudes towards immigration in the class and for the population	Student generated data; British Social Attitudes (BSA)
Politics of Policy Making (Politics)	Tutorial on 'Agenda setting' relating public opinion to data from the Speech from the Throne	UK Policy Agendas Project
Sociology Dissertation (Sociology)	Lecture, guidebook and drop-in sessions to Support students to use quantitative data in their dissertations	UK Data Service, Census; British Social Attitudes Information System
Year 2 (2013/2014)		
British Society and Culture (Sociology)	Embedding data on ethnicity and class inequalities into lecture and tutorial materials	2011 Census; Neighbourhood Statistics; Gapminder; OECD
Urban Sociology (Sociology)	Embedding in lectures and tutorial and identifying sources of data for students to use in coursework	Neighbourhood statistics
Research and study skills (Politics)	Workshops on inequality and civic participation examining attitudinal and behaviour differences	Student data; British Social Attitudes (BSA); British Election Studies (BES)
Politics Project (Politics)	Student led survey on attitudes towards immigration, including experiments in question wording	Student generated data
Racism & Ethnicity in the UK (Sociology)	Identified relevant data to embed in lectures or tutorials	2011 Census; Dynamics of diversity: Evidence from the 2011 census ESRC Centre on Dynamics of Ethnicity
The Sociology of Spirituality (Sociology)	Identified relevant data to embed in lectures or tutorials	World Values Survey (WVS); Office for National Statistics (ONS); Pew Research Center
Gender Sexuality and Cultures (Sociology)	Identified relevant data to embed in lectures or tutorials	The National Survey of Sexual Attitudes and Lifestyles; British Social Attitudes; OECD
Work, Economy & Society (Sociology)	Identified areas for embedding quantitative data	–

the basis for a linked tutorial built around how attitudes towards immigration vary between the students in the class and the British public.

In this model, statistical concepts and techniques are implicit to the exercise but the focus is on answering substantively interesting questions. Students tend to show high levels of engagement with data measuring their attitudes and how they, as a group, vary from the general population. In turn, seeing such attitudinal differences emerge helps students to appreciate the problems of generalising from their own experiences and to think about the social processes producing such differences. The exercise enables a host of related and methodologically important concerns related to survey design to be considered in context as they arise. By mimicking the research process, the exercise enables conversations about the limitations of data and the process through which it is generated. For instance, students can input their own experience of answering the questions, when discussing if the questions measure attitudes reliably.

Hands-on with data

In another first year politics course unit, students develop a small research project or proposal based around a substantive theme selected for each year (examples include inequality and civic participation). This is again linked to relevant questions from national surveys but rather than providing students with the national results in the form of prepared tables, we developed a practical computer workshop in which students access the survey data using online interfaces.[2] Students can use these online interfaces without prior software training in a data analysis package such as SPSS. They therefore offer a rare opportunity to incorporate hands-on data work into a substantive course where there may be limited timetable space and access to computer clusters. A single hour session using these interfaces saw students confidently generate and download bespoke tables for a range of variables. The practical workshop also guided students to compare population sub-groups using simple cross-tabulations and to source data for their project work. By enabling students to work hands-on with real data early in their studies interest is engaged and confidence built, preparing students for more formal training in data analysis. In this case, the clear link to formally assessed work is important for meaningful change necessitating engagement with quantitative material. This in turn, raises the need to ensure that the associated skill set is explicitly written into learning outcomes, both at the unit and course level.

An empirical evidence base to critique theory

A further effective approach to embedding is to provide an empirical evidence base to support critical engagement with theories presented in the substantive course unit. This approach was used in several course units. The first teaching partnerships to use such an activity related to a level 1 course unit on the sociology of personal life, taken by single- and joint-honours students in Sociology. The collaboration created materials for use in a lecture and tutorial on 'living alone'. Based on data from the UK social survey Understanding Society, a series of tables gave insight into the characteristics of those living alone and how they compare to those living in other household arrangements. Along with the theoretical background provided by the lecture and tutorial reading, this empirical evidence supports discussion around the topics of stigma, stereotypes and social norms and how they connect with gender and life stage.

With a clear focus on the substantive questions being addressed, the tutorial exercise introduces students to quantitative data as an integral part of sociological study. Students are engaged in learning and applying key quantitative concepts and skills such as reading percentage tables which can be extended by, for example, showing how to calculate ratios as an aid to making comparisons. The tutorial also provides opportunity to discuss key methodological issues by asking students to critically reflect on the measurement and categorisation of living arrangements, socio-economic classifications and concepts such as life satisfaction. Having used the data to profile the characteristics of those living alone, we can ask students to reflect on the reasons for the patterns observed and how they relate to theoretical ideas they are learning. In this way, analytical concepts such as association and causality can be introduced with reference to real data and to the substantive theme. If suitable, these critical reflections can provide a useful context to introduce more challenging ideas, for example, showing some of the tables with confidence intervals added can facilitate the discussion of statistical significance.

To support the embedding activity, we developed explicit learning outcomes for both class activities (very concrete) and for chunks of learning (more abstract). We found the use of explicit learning outcomes helpful in two ways. First, it helped teaching assistants and lecturers to work in a team focused upon the agreed objectives of each activity. Second, it helped students realise what a strong performance would look like to the teacher. Whilst theory is important in sociology, it became possible to say precisely what would be valued in introducing empirical data or a critique of measurement into an essay or exam. In the end, it was possible to increase the expectation that students should include empirical evidence in their essays or exams.

The teaching partnership for a final year Sociology course unit *Power and Protest* provides a further example of this model of embedding. In this partnership, we worked with the lecturer to develop an evidence pack for a class debate in a week of the course focused on political participation and apathy. We provided students with a range of empirical data with which to discuss and critique different theoretical positions from a preceding lecture. This evidence pack took comprised a time series of simple tabulations of survey measures of participation cross-tabulated by age, sourced from selected surveys including BSA. The data showed various patterns in political participation and, as a result, students gained experience of selecting appropriate evidence to form an argument and the multi-dimensionality of complex concepts such as political engagement. In the second year of running the workshop, we added the task of sourcing evidence using the online interfaces discussed earlier. This independent activity, which was supported with a guidebook, provided students with an opportunity work hands-on with the original data sources and to practise skills relating to the sourcing and presentation of evidence.

The examples discussed here share obvious similarities. Central to all is the inclusion of empirical data to enrich teaching on substantive themes. In our teaching partnerships, we draw heavily on the wealth of UK social survey data, which can be accessed free of charge under academic licence from the UK Data Service. Additionally, the use of online tools has enabled both staff and students to access data without needing to use statistical packages. Outputs engage students in some common QM learning activities but also address learning objectives relating to measurement, comparison and the relationship between theory and evidence. When repeated across course units, these forms of embedding can help establish familiarity with quantitative approaches while developing confidence in the basic skills required of a critical reader of quantitative evidence. This embedded approach is therefore giving the important subject-specific opportunities for reflective learning on the strengths and limitations of quantitative data and methods to a field of study.

Evaluation of embedding

In our collaborative model of embedding, we have tried to assess initiatives from the perspective of all communities of practice involved. This evaluation process incorporates reflective practice and more formal methods including staff interviews and student surveys and focus groups. We use this process to continually inform revision of materials and approaches to curriculum innovation.

First, reflections on the partnerships and embedding activities by the project team have produced several outcomes that are important to note. A foremost positive outcome is that the collaborative partnerships produced materials that have been used, re-used and further adapted. Not all proposed partnerships came to fruition or led to successful quantitative embedding. In our case, the voluntary partnerships did not experience any of the resistance to including quantitative materials that Falkingham and McGowan (2011, p. 114) had found using a similar model. Instead, the two main barriers we encountered were competing time pressures on staff and staff leaving the institution. However, an unexpected but positive outcome was that the project engendered additional interest from teaching staff not originally involved. In general, preparing materials for embedding work is time consuming and collaborative partnership working required the dedicated time of the project team. Thus, the additional interest quickly emphasised the challenge of developing sustainable strategies for resourcing such activities beyond the set-up funding period. One method we tried was to employ Social Statistics Ph.D. students to source data and develop materials under the guidance of the partner lectures. This provided an effective and highly flexible model with which to respond to increases and variation in demand across the academic year but still required significant financial resources (typically around 20 h of research assistant time per module).

While acknowledging the resource intensive nature of this type of curriculum development, we are finding that once successfully incorporated within a curriculum, embedding activities can be sustained without major re-investment of resources. Most of our interventions have re-run with minimal involvement of the project team and, in some cases, even following changes to the course convenor. We did, however, experience some difficulties in the re-use of embedding activities with new staff needing the aims and outcomes to be clarified. This problem has perhaps been most acute with teaching assistants taking tutorials or seminars on the larger course units. From our experience, features that appear to support the longevity of embedding materials are clearly specified activities with specific learning outcomes that can be understood by new convenors, and where applicable the teaching assistants. However, it may also be that in some circumstances ongoing support and training is required.

Finally, our project suggests there are limits on the types of quantitative data and methods that can be embedded. As the examples show, our embedding activities incorporate only basic level numerical tasks, with the emphasis on critically interpreting data. Rather than reflecting any explicit decision to avoid introducing more difficult QM topics, such as regression, the nature of embedding activities results from individual decisions made through the collaborative partnerships about what would be appropriate for the specific teaching context. A number of the partner lecturers stressed the limited availability of time and space within the unit curriculum, and felt that it would be difficult to increase the level of statistical content without sacrifices to the existing substantive content. A further concern expressed was whether students would have the prerequisites to work with more advanced QM concepts and methods, especially as course units in Politics and Sociology attract students from other disciplines and schools.

In terms of student evaluation, our use of questionnaires for each of the partner course units encountered problems of low response rates. In particular, attempts to use online surveys were particularly unsuccessful and, as a result, our evaluation data comes from a small selection of course units where data was collected using paper based questionnaires. The questionnaires were distributed and completed during a lecture or tutorial in the last teaching week of the course unit. This approach to data collection produced much better response rates but the samples consist only of students attending the classes. We obtained 73 completed questionnaires from students in three course units. Response rates reflect the proportion of students completing questionnaires within each class and range between 53 and 80%, see note to Table 2 for further details. While acknowledging that our data is not fully representative of the student body, it affirms that the initiative has been well received in the classroom. Table 2 shows that the majority of students surveyed have positive responses to quantitative embedding and that they appreciate the use of well-selected examples to help them learn about both quantitative research and substantive theory.

There was clear support for including quantitative training in social science degree programmes. Only 1 in 5 agreed that social science students should not have to study statistics, and 4 in 5 indicated that learning quantitative skills was a useful part of a degree programme. As Figure 1 shows, students agree that learning to interpret quantitative data and topics can provide a range of benefits related to academic study (forming convincing arguments, doing research and making a subject more interesting) and beyond (understanding statistics in the media and getting a good job). These themes also emerged in the qualitative feedback with students emphasising the presence of numerical data in other aspects of life:

> When you're getting out of university and going forward a lot of what you're doing is looking a numbers and having to make a judgement. Your world is not going to be devoid of numbers. It is important and would be valuable addition to a degree.

Focusing on quantitative embedding, student feedback has been primarily positive towards both principal and practice. The qualitative evidence especially points towards students recognising a preference for contextualised encounters within quantitative evidence.

> Integrated into what you are doing so it doesn't feel like you're doing quantitative data for quantitative data's sake. Say in politics there is a really important survey that is related to exactly what we're learning about and then you say were going to interpret this in this way; then it doesn't really feel like we're doing it because it's so interlinked and that's the point of quantitative data any way, that it's just done as part of all your other research.

Moreover, students report finding the use of data helpful in bringing theories alive and making them seem less abstract. The majority of surveyed students agreed that the embedded content helped them to make sense of the theory and that it related to the main topics well. Similarly a student on the *Power and Protest* course unit commented:

> I found it extremely useful to learn about the theory and then have some real life contextual evidence to engage with – it makes the theories feel more worthwhile learning about. Sometimes I feel that it is easy to forget that the theories we learn about in

Table 2. Student attitudes towards quantitative data and methods in their degree.

	Strongly agree	Agree	Neither agree nor disagree	Disagree	Strongly disagree	Not sure	Total
Quantitative data helped me make sense of the theory	8.2	60.3	24.7	5.5	0	1.4	100
It was difficult to understand the quantitative data	2.7	16.4	21.9	47.9	11	0	100
I enjoyed looking at the numbers	5.5	21.9	46.6	20.5	5.5	0	100
The quantitative data distracted from the main topic	2.8	11.1	30.6	47.2	8.3	0	100
The quantitative data related to the main topics well	7	62	28.2	2.8	0	0	100
Seeing tables and graphs has helped me to feel more confident looking at numbers	2.8	5.6	38.9	45.8	6.9	0	100
More quantitative data should be used in teaching	8.2	38.4	30.1	20.5	1.4	1.4	100
I don't think social science students should have to study statistics	4.1	15.1	17.8	45.2	16.4	1.4	100
Learning to interpret and analyse numerical data is a useful part of a degree	21.9	56.2	15.1	4.1	1.4	1.4	100
I am interested in learning how to interpret and use quantitative data	13.7	42.5	17.8	20.5	2.7	2.7	100

Notes: $N = 73$, The data derived from a survey of students from three course units within Sociology and Politics at the University of Manchester. The survey took place in either a lecture or tutorial at the end of the semester, following all embedding activities. For 1 unit large unit, data comes from three tutorial groups with the following response rates Group $A = 60\%$, Group B = 80% and Group C = 67%. For other two course units, data comes from the whole class with response rates of 69 and 53%. The response rates primarily reflect non-attendance by students.
Darker cells indicate more common responses.

lectures are actually real life issues that really do effect the way that people live their lives, their opinions and actions.

These attitudes and perceptions of students indicate that the teaching partnerships can successfully develop quantitative materials that reinforce existing learning outcomes.

While nearly all students surveyed indicated that there were benefits to learning quantitative skills, a minority were less favourable about their experience of

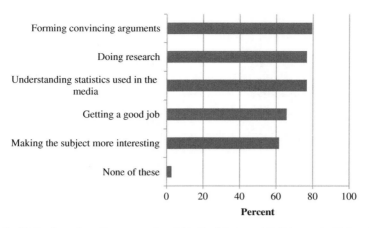

N=73, Students from 3 course units within Sociology and Politics at the University of Manchester, see table 2 for details of the sample.

Figure 1. Student views of the benefits of learning quantitative skills.
Notes: Percentage of students indicating that 'Learning to interpret and analyse quantitative data can help with … '. $N = 73$, Students from three course units within Sociology and Politics at the University of Manchester, see Table 2 for details of the sample

quantitative embedding. For instance, nearly 20% of surveyed students indicated they found the quantitative element difficult to understand, 25% did not enjoy the new activities and 13% found they distracted from the main course unit themes. In one of the focus groups, a student explained how they missed a seminar because they felt ill-prepared as a result of being unable to calculate a percentage. These evaluation findings underline how some students will feel challenged and potentially isolated by the inclusion of quantitative data in the curriculum. Such a finding has varied implications for embedding. On the one-hand, quantitative embedding is potentially the best approach to supporting students likely to struggle, especially when teaching partnerships utilise the skills of both QM experts and substantive teachers to present quantitative training in an accessible and engaging way. However, the repeating of quantitative content could help to alienate students struggling with high levels of statistical anxiety (Slootmaeckers et al., 2014).

We have been monitoring the impact of the curriculum change on student decisions to further engage with quantitative data. We have long been aware that despite training students in the skills needed to conduct quantitative research in their dissertations very few students opt to do this in their final year dissertations. For the 2011–2012 academic year, an audit of dissertations in Politics and Sociology confirmed the perception by revealing that just one student had undertaken a quantitative dissertation. Encouragingly, a similar audit two years later indicated the number opting for secondary quantitative analysis had increased to 15 (out of 118). Similarly, there has also been a gradual increase in the number of students taking further quantitative options in their third year of study including a new third year course on modelling inequality using regression (with enrolment going up from 7 to nearly 30 in its second year of running).

Adopting the embedded QM model: challenges and opportunities

Our project focused on solutions to the challenges of teaching quantitative methods in one institution. In this final section, we use our experiences to consider the challenges and opportunities others might face in adopting a similar model of embedding. First we argue that an embedded approach to QM learning requires change not only among methods teachers and not only at the level of individual course units. Within departments and at programme level, non-methods teaching staff need to buy into the benefits of embedding and the contribution of QM in their subject area. They must also be prepared and able to invest scarce time on the revision of course units, which they may feel are already adequate. Crucially, there must also be a willingness among substantive social science teachers and QM experts to collaborate.

Meeting the first of these conditions is likely to be much harder in some institutions, depending upon the particular methodological traditions and the extent to which there are QM specialists within teaching groups. The University of Manchester is in a relatively advantaged position as we can draw on a history of inter-disciplinary collaboration between Sociology, Politics and Social Statistics, as well data expertise in the UK Data Service and now the British Election Study (BES) and Q-Step team. In institutional settings where QM is more marginalised in research and teaching, initiatives of the type may be much harder to implement, even extending to some resistance on intellectual grounds (Platt, 2012). Given the strongly qualitative traditions of many departments and wariness, if not resistance, to the teaching and use of quantitative methods, it is crucial that initiatives such as the Manchester project are not seen as attempts to impose QM or to suggest that QM approaches are epistemologically or methodological superior to other positions.[3] Rather, we argue that basic quantitative skills are essential for any social scientist to understand and make an informed critique of research contributions to a field. Moreover, we also emphasise how in a period when many social science departments are looking to extend the QM training provided in undergraduate degrees, a response that focuses only on methods teaching risks exacerbating the current problems of students feeling disconnected and alienated from methods. From our experiences, a model of collaborative teaching partnerships offers a promising vehicle for this interpretation of embedding as the substantive content of the course remains pivotal.

Resources are undoubtedly a key constraint in adopting an embedded model. The development of engaging materials for embedding requires time and expertise, and it is an important question whether this approach is replicable without dedicated grant or other funding. For most HE lecturers, time for course development can be hard to prioritise against competing demands. We argue, therefore, that curriculum development needs to be built more explicitly into work allocation models and incentivised. Within the current context, however, an advantage of our model of embedding is that curriculum change is incremental: innovations can be focused on specific course units, even just a specific topic, lecture or seminar. As a result, embedding can be part of a routine process of course unit revision as convenors perceive a need for change or opportunity for improvement.

A sustainable strategy for embedding must identify ways to support collaboration and the sharing of expertise. In our case, the Manchester Q-Step programme will support quantitatively trained staff to continue embedding activities. However, we recognise that the presence of quantitatively trained staff varies across institutions;

as is the extent to which those with QM expertise are integrated within departmental teaching cultures. QM specialists often collaborate in research with QM skilled staff from other schools or institutions and, as teachers of methods courses, can be isolated in their teaching. In such a context, our model of embedding may initially be limited to small-scale local adoptions, which if successful could be the catalyst for bringing together new collaborations, especially where supported by changes at the institutional level. Institutional level changes might include organisational changes to ensure substantive and methods teaching staff come together in teaching groups, as well as offering more formal opportunities to collaborate through greater use of 'team teaching' models, both within and across discipline areas.

The resources needed for embedding suggest Open Educational Resources (OERs) could be instrumental. The benefits are especially great in teaching environments where QM expertise is lacking but they could be much wider since the sourcing and preparing of embedding materials is resource intensive. For instance, as Falkingham and McGowan (2011) highlight, certain topics and themes (such as immigration, globalisation and poverty) are widespread throughout social science curriculums. Thus, some up-to-date, accessible and engaging material relating to such topics could be relevant across a large number of teaching contexts. There is already a sizable repository of excellent QM focused OERs (Carter, 2011, 2012);[4] however, they predominately cover data analysis, and are therefore less useful resources for quantitative embedding. OERs designed for embedding are however becoming more common, following initiatives such as ESRC's Curriculum Innovation and Researcher Development Initiatives, including case studies and teaching materials from our own project.[5]

Conclusion

We have outlined a specific, institutional response to the problem of teaching QM to undergraduate social scientists. To make the concepts more relevant to their substantive interests, we suggest that quantitative data, concepts and methods be integrated into existing course units and not just taught separately as 'methods'. To achieve this, we suggest a framework that emphasises collaborative teaching where the experience and skills of both substantive lecturers and methods lecturers can be harnessed to provide a well-conceived and coherent programme of study for students. One project such as ours will not address the UK QM skills shortage alone. We describe a model for embedding QM in teaching that could be adapted and adopted in other HE institutions if the challenges identified in the paper can be addressed.

Acknowledgement

The authors gratefully acknowledge the support of the Economic and Social Research Council through grants received under the Researcher Development Initiative and the Curriculum Innovation Initiative [grant numbers ES/J011665/1 and ES/J011622/1].

Disclosure statement

No potential conflict of interest was reported by the authors.

Notes

1. See Heuvel-Panhuizen and Van den Drijvers (2014) for more on RME and Searle and Barmby (2012) for an evaluation of an RME teaching approach in the UK.

2. The BSA Information System at http://www.britsocat.com/ and the British Election Study Information System at http://www.besis.org/.
3. This is a worry expressed by, amongst others, Byrne (2012).
4. See for example, Jorum (http://www.jorum.ac.uk/); ESRC's Quantitative Methods Initiative (http://www.quantitativemethods.ac.uk/); OPOSSEM, the Online Portal for Social Science Education in Methodology (http://opossem.org/), and; the Oxford Social Science QM teaching archive (http://www.sociology.ox.ac.uk/qm-teaching-materials-archive).
5. Case studies and teaching materials from the project are available online under Creative Common's license (http://www.socialsciences.manchester.ac.uk/essted).

References

Adeney, K., & Carey, S. (2011). How to teach the reluctant and terrified to love statistics: The importance of context in teaching quantitative methods in the social sciences. In G. Payne & M. Williams (Eds.), *Teaching quantitative methods: Getting the basics right* (pp. 157–176). London: Sage.

Askew, M., Brown, M., Rhodes, V., Johnson, D., & Wiliam, D. (1997). *Effective teachers of numeracy.* London: Kings College.

Bloom, B., Englehart, M., Furst, E., Hill, W., & Krathwohl, D. (1956). *Taxonomy of educational objectives: The classification of educational goals. Handbook I: Cognitive domain.* New York, NY: David McKay Company.

Byrne, D. (2012). UK sociology and quantitative methods: Are we as weak as they think? Or Are they barking up the wrong tree? *Sociology, 46,* 13–24.

Carter, J. (2011). Jorum: A national service for learning and teaching. In G. Payne & M. Williams (Eds.), *Teaching quantitative methods: Getting the basics right* (pp. 157–176). London: Sage.

Carter, J. (2012). How OERs can help a strategically important and vulnerable subject area – Quantitative social science. *Journal of Interactive Media in Education, 2012*(2). doi: 10.5334/2012-16

Chamberlain, M. J., Hillier, J., & Signoretta, P. (2014). Counting better? An examination of the impact of quantitative method teaching on statistical anxiety and confidence. *Active Learning in Higher Education, 16*, 51–66. doi:10.1177/1469787414558983

Falkingham, J., & McGowan, T. (2011). Improving the teaching of quantitative methods to undergraduate social scientists: Understanding and overcoming the barriers. In G. Payne & M. Williams (Eds.), *Teaching quantitative methods: Getting the basics right* (pp. 99–120). London: Sage.

Hampden-Thompson, G., & Sundaram, V. (2013). Developing quantitative research skills and conceptualising an integrated approach to teaching research methods to education students. *The AISHE-J: All Ireland Journal of Teaching and Learning in Higher Education, 5*, 901–924.

Heuvel-Panhuizen, M., & Van den Drijvers, P. (2014). Realistic Mathematics Education. In S. Lerman (Ed.), *Encyclopedia of mathematics education* (pp. 521–525). Dordrecht: Springer.

Hodgen, J., Pepper, D., & London, C. (2010). *Is the UK an outlier?* London: Nuffield Foundation.

Howery, C. B., & Havidan, R. (2006). Integrating data analysis (IDA): Working with sociology departments to address the quantitative literacy gap. *Teaching Sociology, 34*, 23–38.

MacInnes, J. (2009). *Final report: Proposals to support and improve the teaching of quantitative research methods at undergraduate level in the UK.* Swindon: Economic and Social Research Council.

Parker, J., Dobson, A., Scott, S., Wyman, M., & Landén, A. S. (2008). *International benchmarking review of best practice in the provision of undergraduate teaching in quantitative methods in the social sciences* (pp. 1–91). Staffordshire: Keele University.

Payne, G., Williams, M., & Chamberlin, S. (2004). Methodological pluralism in British sociology. *Sociology, 38*, 153–163.

Platt, J. (2012). Making them count: How effective has official encouragement of quantitative methods been in British sociology? *Current Sociology, 60*, 690–704. doi:10.1177/0011392112440438

Searle, J., & Barmby, P. (2012). *Evaluation report on the realistic mathematics education pilot project at Manchester Metropolitan University.* Durham. Retrieved from http://www.mei.org.uk/files/pdf/rme_evaluation_final_report.pdf

Skemp, R. R. (1976). Relational understanding and instrumental understanding. *Mathematics Teaching, 77*, 20–26.

Slootmaeckers, K., Kerremans, B., & Adriaensen, J. (2014). Too afraid to learn: Attitudes towards statistics as a barrier to learning statistics and to acquiring quantitative skills. *Politics, 34*, 91–200. doi:10.1111/1467-9256.12042

Vygotsky, L. S. (1987). *Thinking and speech. The collected works of L.S. Vygotsky*, Vol. 1. New York, NY: Plenum.

Vygotsky, L. S. (1998). Development of thinking and the formation of concepts in the adolescent. In R. W. Rieber (Ed.), *The collected works of L. S. Vygotsky* (Vol. 2, Chapter 2, pp. 29–81). New York, NY: Plenum.

Wathan, J., Brown, M., & Williamson, L. (2011). Understanding and overcoming the barriers increasing secondary analysis in undergraduate dissertations. In J. Payne & M. Williams (Eds.), *Teaching quantitative methods: Getting the basics right* (pp. 121–141). London: Sage.

Wenger, E. (1999). *Communities of practice: Learning meaning and identity.* Cambridge: Cambridge University Press.

Wiles, R., Durrant, G., De Broe, S., & Powell, J. (2009). Methodological approaches at PhD and skills sought for research posts in academia: A mismatch? *International Journal of Social Research Methodology, 12*, 257–269. doi:10.1080/13645570701708550

Williams, M., Payne, G., Hodgkinson, L., & Poade, D. (2008). Does british sociology count? Sociology students' attitudes toward quantitative methods. *Sociology, 42*, 1003–1021. doi:10.1177/0038038508094576

Williams, M., & Sutton, C. (2011). Challenges and opportunities for developing teaching in quantitative methods. In G. Payne & M. Williams (Eds.), *Teaching quantitative methods: Getting the basics right* (pp. 66–84). London: Sage.

Teaching social research methods after the critical turn: challenges and benefits of a constructivist pedagogy

Cosmo Howard[a] and Michelle Brady[b]

[a]School of Government and International Relations, Griffith University, Brisbane, Australia; [b]School of Social Science, University of Queensland, Brisbane, Australia

> An increasing challenge for teaching methods courses in the social sciences is the 'critical turn', which has encouraged some students to adopt an anti-empirical orientation. We present a case study of a compulsory undergraduate methods course in a political science department strongly influenced by post-structuralist philosophies. The first author redesigned the course to implement four constructivist pedagogical principles: (1) develop a full understanding of students' pre-existing perceptions of political science research methods; (2) encourage students to see methodology as an inevitably contested field; (3) provide space for students to choose a methodological approach that best aligns with their personal stance on knowledge; and (4) encourage students to view research as an ongoing 'conversation'. We critically reflect on the implementation of these constructivist pedagogical strategies and argue they improve students' critical engagement with course material, increase linkages between methods teaching and other disciplinary subject matter, and accommodate diverse student perspectives and needs.

Introduction

Research methodology courses are among the most challenging in university teaching (Earley, 2014; Wagner, Garner, & Kawulich, 2011). Students commonly feel such courses are dull and irrelevant to their needs, due to the abstractness of the content (Blalock, 1987; Bridges, Gillmore, Pershing, & Bates, 1998; Earley, 2014). In addition, methods courses are often more intellectually demanding than subject matter courses because they require students to grasp complex abstract principles and processes, and assessment items are more commonly located at the top of Bloom's hierarchy of educational objectives (i.e. application). Research suggests these higher demands generate methods anxiety among students, leading them to avoid methodology courses (Blalock, 1987; Bridges et al., 1998; Earley, 2014). Students' general aversion to methodology courses is problematic because the ability to conduct primary research and the capacity to distinguish credible empirical claims from invalid assertions should be some of the most important practical skills students take away from their studies in the social sciences (Marfleet & Dille, 2005; Ryan, Saunders, Rainsford, & Thompson, 2014).

In this paper we focus on a new challenge associated with teaching social research methods – namely the impact of the 'critical turn' (Burawoy, 2005, p. 313)

– and we ask how this new problem, as well as existing challenges, can be addressed using a constructivist pedagogy. We use the notion of the critical turn to refer to recent influential scholarship in the social sciences that draws on post-modern and post-structural critiques of conventional research methods (Bacchi, 2009; Bang & Esmark, 2007; Fischer, 2009; Hajer, 2003; Lloyd & Thacker, 1997; Schmidt, 2008). Such critical approaches have made significant inroads in disciplines including anthropology, criminology, education, geography, political science and sociology (Hay, 2002; Lloyd & Thacker, 1997). The challenge of the critical turn for methods teaching is that it can encourage students to be actively sceptical of the value of learning empirical research methodologies, and thus it potentially compounds the existing problems of methods anxiety and student disinterest.

Our claim is that a constructivist pedagogy, which at its core means students are enabled and required to construct their own learning experiences (Richardson, 2003), is of particular value for teaching introductory social-scientific methodology courses in contexts where students are coming to the course material with a strong degree of scepticism about empirical research. A constructivist approach to teaching methods helps address the concerns of critically inclined students while also catering for the preferences of students interested in traditional methodologies. It foregrounds students' existing anxieties and assumptions about learning social research methods, and empowers them to choose the methodological approaches that fit their academic needs and intellectual priorities. While constructivism is particularly useful for teaching methods to critically oriented students, our findings also have general implications for teaching methods in social science. The constructivist approach assists with the important goal of integrating methods into the curriculum (Dyrhauge, 2014; Leston-Bandeira, 2013; Ryan et al., 2014) by explicitly framing methodological concepts in relation to students' disciplinary backgrounds. Furthermore, the constructivist approach facilitates the development of more critical approaches to studying research methods in all students, including greater self-reflection among students influenced by the critical turn.

We base our arguments in this paper on the findings of a reflective case study of a compulsory methods course for third year undergraduates undertaking the honours program in a political science department on the vanguard of the critical turn, at a medium-sized Canadian public research university. The course was redesigned and taught by the first author during his initial years as an assistant professor, beginning in 2006. Using the reflective case method (Navarro, 2005; Oldland, 2011; Yan, 2013) and data drawn from this author's personal journals and teaching notes, the paper sets out the rationale for redesigning the course, the key design principles of the course, and the outcomes over a period of three years.

The paper begins with a brief outline of the critical turn, and then explores its influence in the first author's political science department. The following sections review the literature on teaching research methods in the social sciences, and constructivist pedagogy. After this, the reflective case method used in the study is described, followed by a discussion of the research findings.

The critical turn in the social sciences

As we will illustrate below, the 'critical turn' has strongly shaped how undergraduate students in some social science departments interpret and engage with courses on social research methods. By the critical turn, we are specifically referring to developments beginning in the 1970s that challenged established practices in and attitudes towards the social sciences. Critical theorists argued that the positivistic assumptions of the natural sciences were inappropriate for the study of social and political life because they ignored human agency and served to hide the ideological biases of authors. Second-wave feminists took up such ideas in work on the gendered assumptions underlying mainstream sociology and political science (Weedon, 1997). Critical theory also provided the philosophical foundations for the radical challenges to established methods posed by post-modernist and post-structuralist writers beginning in the 1970s (Hay, 2002). Among these, Michel Foucault most directly addressed the problematic nature of 'scientific' claims in social analyses by explicitly showing how academic disciplines selectively legitimize knowledges while denying the right of certain actors to speak with authority (Burawoy, 2005).

These points highlight that the contemporary critical turn is not primarily or exclusively about the use of academic research to criticise problems in the 'outside world' or to advocate for 'emancipatory projects' (for such an interpretation see Hammersley, 2005, p. 175). Rather, the critical turn folds critical analysis back on scholarship itself, and attempts to illuminate how both objectivist and emancipatory approaches to research depend upon and solidify power relations (Hay, 2002).

The critical turn has had a discernible but varied impact on social scientific practice (Hay, 2002). Foucault's ideas have attained significant popularity in political science, sociology, anthropology, geography and women's studies (Lloyd & Thacker, 1997). At the same time, much research in the social sciences proceeds untouched by these post-structuralist ideas. Although interest in critical and interpretive methods is growing in political science (Yanow & Schwartz-Shea, 2013), positivism and quantitative methods continue to hold sway in most of the top-ranked departments and journals, particularly in the United States (Hay, 2002). Furthermore, the critical turn has inspired numerous counter-reactions in the form of 'new hegemonic projects based on the supremacy of quantification or rational choice theory' (Burawoy, 2005, p. 317).

The result is a split between positivist social science scholars, who accept pretensions to objectivity and seek increasingly sophisticated, mostly quantitative tools to establish causality, and a new generation of scholars trained in critical approaches (Burawoy, 2005), who seek to problematize such practices and who have tended to eschew conventional empirical studies and methods such as surveys, interviewing and observation in favour of critical discursive analysis of texts and talk (Lloyd & Thacker, 1997). This division has clear implications for those instructors charged with introducing students to what it means to conduct social science research in practice.

Teaching social research methods

The existing research literature presents a negative picture of students' experiences with social research methods courses and suggests that undergraduates commonly feel such courses are irrelevant to their lives; they are anxious about the content and 'uninterested and therefore unmotivated to learn the material' (Earley, 2014, p. 245). When they enter these courses students have 'poor attitudes' (Earley, 2014, p. 246) and misconceptions about research. However, existing research does not identify when students develop these problematic attitudes and dispositions towards research methods (Earley, 2014). Although, as Earley (2014) argues, there is a literature on teaching strategies that increase students' engagement with research methods courses (including active learning, problem based learning, service learning, and experiential learning), research has largely ignored the specific course content, learning goals and assessment plans of research methods courses and how these might contribute to student disengagement. Furthermore, Wagner et al. (2011) suggest little progress has been made in determining the traits of an effective methods teacher, the challenges specific to teaching particular methodologies, and how teaching research methods differs across disciplines. A series of studies identify a lack of pedagogical culture amongst research methods instructors (Kilburn, Nind, & Wiles, 2014; Wagner et al., 2011). Methods courses are said to lack 'the exchange of ideas within a climate of systematic debate, investigation and evaluation surrounding all aspects of teaching and learning in the subject' (Wagner et al., 2011, p. 75).

Although there is little existing research on social research methods pedagogies, evidence suggests that instructors would like to improve their pedagogy (Kilburn et al., 2014). Furthermore, Kilburn et al.'s (2014) comprehensive review of the literature suggests there is significant agreement on some pedagogical goals, with most studies recommending that instructors:

(1) make the research process visible by actively engaging students in aspects of the methods at hand; [and]
(2) facilitate learning through the experience of conducting research (Kilburn et al., 2014, p. 197)

However, considerably fewer studies recommended that instructors 'encourage critical reflection on research practice' rather than simply transmit 'technical or procedural knowledge' (Kilburn et al., 2014, p. 197).

There is a small body of literature on teaching methods in political science (Dyrhauge, 2014; Leston-Bandeira, 2013; Marfleet & Dille, 2005; Parker, 2010; Ryan et al., 2014; Schwartz-Shea, 2003; Wagner et al., 2011). This research consistently finds that methods receive limited attention in Anglo-American undergraduate political science programs (Parker, 2010). Some have documented a systematic bias towards positivist and quantitative approaches and neglect of critical, interpretivist and qualitative approaches in political science, compared to other social science disciplines (Schwartz-Shea, 2003; Wagner et al., 2011). Nevertheless, as in other disciplines, political science students are anxious about methods courses, bored by the content and impatient about methods teaching that is not immediately and obviously useful for their study or employment (Dyrhauge, 2014; Leston-Bandeira, 2013; Marfleet & Dille, 2005; Ryan et al., 2014). Political science instructors tend to avoid methods courses as well. As a result, such courses are often taught by junior untenured faculty, who have to juggle heavy teaching and research loads, or senior faculty with limited enthusiasm for innovative teaching models (Ryan et al., 2014). The result is that many political science methods courses are often 'not treated seriously', but rather as an 'add on' to the existing curriculum and 'rigid' set of skills that need to be transmitted to reluctant students (Ryan et al., 2014). Evidence also suggests these traditional approaches to political science methods teaching lead to poor student satisfaction and sub-optimal learning outcomes (Leston-Bandeira, 2013; Marfleet & Dille, 2005; Ryan et al., 2014).

Relevance of constructivist pedagogy for teaching social research methods

Constructivist pedagogy challenges the existing transmission-based models for teaching social science methods described by Kilburn et al. (2014) and others. Advocates of constructivist pedagogies reject the idea that instructors should simply aim to transmit technical information to build learners' repositories of universal objective knowledge. Instructors, they argue, should focus on students' existing mental constructions regarding the course content (Richardson, 2003; Tenenbaum, Naidu, Jegede, & Austin, 2001). Constructivists argue that students' subject matter knowledge should be viewed as an 'entity that is mentally constructed via the actions and experiences that the learner undergoes with the immediate learning and broader social environments' (Tenenbaum et al., 2001, p. 89). Learning occurs when 'individuals create their own new understandings on the basis of an interaction between what they already know and believe and ideas and knowledge with which they come into contact' (Richardson, 2003, p. 1624). Each learner will develop an idiosyncratic understanding that depends in part on the existing mental constructs held. Furthermore, the meaning that students develop may be shaped by their classroom peers, cohort or school if this provides them 'the opportunity to share and provide warrant for these meanings' (Richardson, 2003, p. 1625). Learning occurs not when students simply absorb preexisting knowledge but instead 'through the establishment of malleable mental constructs' (Tenenbaum et al., 2001, p. 89). As such, the role of the instructor is to help create an environment where students can continually adapt their existing mental schema to develop a more reflective understanding of the methods that underpin knowledge (Tenenbaum et al., 2001). Specific learning strategies include a learner-centred ethos, opportunities for learners to reflect on personal experiences, learner-learner interaction, opportunities for learners to 'think aloud', and development of thinking skills (Tenenbaum et al., 2001, p. 95).

From this perspective, effective learning about research methods emerges from opportunities for 'reflections and personal insight' that allow students to build their own schemas and solutions to particular research problems (Spigner-Littles & Chalon, 1999, p. 204). Rather than primarily aiming to assess students against pre-existing standards, a constructivist teacher of research methods aims to provide a space where students can develop their own distinctive understandings of particular methods. Furthermore, students are encouraged to assess the relevance of any particular methodology or method to their own academic and career goals (Spigner-Littles & Chalon, 1999, p. 204). Finally, a constructivist approach to learning methods involves challenging students' existing mental structures by creating a learning environment that is 'active/manipulative, constructive, collaborative, intentional, conversational, conceptualized and reflective' (Tenenbaum et al., 2001, p. 95).

Data and methods

The findings presented in this article are based on a reflective case study of a course that the first author taught in a political science department whose faculty had strongly embraced the critical turn. Reflective case studies are a popular methodology for critically analysing educational practice (Navarro, 2005; Oldland, 2011; Yan, 2013). This approach involves the instructor using their own teaching as a case and then attempting to explore the processes involved in the teaching and linking these to the larger context (Scott, 2014). Reflective case study analysis is designed to generate rigorous scholarly knowledge in a way that can directly inform and improve practice (Oldland, 2011). Data sources typically include the instructor's written notes, and diaries or journals (Hawker, McMillan, & Palermo, 2013; Oldland, 2011).

Following this approach, the first author kept a teaching journal during his first three years following advice from university early career support seminars. Significant additional notes on teaching were kept to inform teaching portfolios required for the annual performance evaluation and tenure processes. These review documents solicit information about the faculty member's pedagogical philosophy, as well as examples of teaching innovations and course development work. We have not included course evaluations or correspondence with students as data for this paper because we did not obtain ethics clearance to use these. To analyse the journal entries and teaching notes, the texts were first re-read and supplemented by 'memory work' to compose narratives (Scott, 2014). We then coded both the memory narratives and notes using thematic codes derived from our review of the literature on constructivist pedagogies and teaching methods.

Case study context

The department providing this course is known for its research strengths in theory, and particularly post-liberal and post-structuralist critique. When the author joined the department in 2005, four out of the five full professors explicitly engaged with Foucault and other post-structuralist thinkers such as Giorgio Agamben, Gilles Deleuze, Jacques Derrida and Donna Haraway. Their research has been highly influential in the fields of political theory and international relations. By contrast, no faculty were actively using quantitative analysis in their research. Most of the non-professoriate faculty drew on 'mainstream' political science approaches such as historical institutionalism and comparative public policy (Marsh & Stoker, 2002) and relied on qualitative methods including in-depth key informant interviews and systematic analyses of documents. The strong complement of critically inclined theorists and complete absence of quantitative researchers was highly unusual among political science departments in the North American context.

Not surprisingly, the impact of the critical turn was also felt in the classroom. Theory received strong treatment in the undergraduate curriculum, most notably via a sequence of three third-year level courses (taking at least one was compulsory for political science majors). These were normally taught by one of the full professors with post-structuralist inclinations, and they introduced post-structuralist reinterpretations of classical political thinkers. In addition, the department's honours program, which was open to students who satisfied the grade cut off, included a specialized course in theory, also taught by one of the full professors with a post-structuralist research focus.

After completing these courses, honours students were then required to undertake the methods course that is the subject of this article. It was the only methods course in the department and therefore the instructor had to assume students had no prior methods training.

The first author took over responsibly for the methods course in his first year as an assistant professor in the department. In the existing course students learned about a range of political science research methodologies and techniques, including surveys, correlation and regression, and qualitative interviewing. The students completing this course were required to complete a dissertation in the year following the course, and the departmental expectation was that the methods course together with a compulsory honours course in political theory would prepare students to carry out their dissertation research. Colleagues and former students expressed concern that the course was not fulfilling its specified role since students were not engaging with the content nor using the methodological techniques in their honours dissertations. As a result, there was an expectation that the author would redesign and update the course to bring it into closer alignment with student needs and improve evaluation scores.

Using a constructivist approach to teach research methods after the critical turn

In this section we address how constructivist principles were used to redesign the political science methods course. Some aspects of the course remained the same: we kept the textbook but changed all the required course-pack readings. Also, we retained the existing delivery format, which appears common among upper-level undergraduate methods courses (Leston-Bandeira, 2013; Ryan et al., 2014): a three hour seminar broken down into a lecture (with some interaction) followed by in-class presentations, discussion of readings and exercises aimed at helping students complete the major course assessment items (a midterm exam and final research design project). The course was redesigned using the following constructivist strategies: (a) develop a full understanding of students' pre-existing mental constructions of social science research methods; (b) emphasise that research methods are inherently contested and political; (c) provide students with meaningful choices between alternative methodologies; and (d) encourage students to view research as a 'conversation'. In the following sections we describe how these principles were operationalized, and summarise the challenges and benefits.

a. *Understanding students' mental constructions about methods*

The first step in implementing a constructivist methods pedagogy was to systematically review the course and gather information about the learning context along with students' existing orientations towards research methods. The existing course was based on a behaviourist approach that aimed to provide students with objective and truthful content (cf. Tenenbaum et al., 2001). Assessment involved testing students against external standards and providing very little space for students' critical self-reflections on methods. Before redesigning the course the first author met with a previous student cohort to establish the students' key concerns and priorities. In our experience of teaching a range of methods courses, students who come to methods courses from a positivist or realist background display the kinds of methods anxiety discussed in the literature (i.e. they are concerned they will be unable to master the often complex concepts and vocabularies associated with social science research methods courses) (Earley, 2014). However, this was not the major cause of student concern in our case. Instead, in part due to their background in critical theory, students were worried that they would be given little opportunity to challenge the material transmitted by the instructor. Specifically, while their previous semester theory course emphasized the normative and political assumptions underlying different paradigms, the methods course suggested that the best approach to researching specific questions in political science could and should be determined by purely objective considerations. Students were also concerned about the 'disproportionate' emphasis on quantitative techniques given that the vast majority did not wish to use statistics in their honours dissertations.

Discussion also revealed that students tended to associate research methods with statistical methods, which reflects a general tendency within political science, where undergraduate programs are more likely to offer courses on quantitative as opposed to qualitative methods.[1] Finally, while many of the students had embraced the critical turn, a significant minority preferred mainstream political science paradigms and were interested in a more traditional discussion of methodologies.

Most pedagogical approaches recommend that instructors be aware of students' backgrounds, so an emphasis on awareness of context is not exclusive to constructivist approaches. What distinguishes constructivism is attention to students' assumptions about and 'constructions' of course content (Richardson, 2003; Tenenbaum et al., 2001). We designed the three strategies presented next not only to build on students' pre-existing knowledge, but also to engage with and challenge how they constructed methods as a field of study and practice.

b. *Framing research methods as inherently contested and political*

A review of the literature on methods suggests that relatively few instructors encourage students to reflect critically on research practice (Kilburn et al., 2014). Our sense is that instructors in methods courses often discourage student criticism on the grounds that students cannot criticise research designs and techniques until they have fully mastered the technical content. This idea was shared in collegial discussions and departmental meetings, though we have not been able to locate published defences of the idea. Due to our adherence to pedagogical constructivism we rejected the assumption that there is one correct interpretation of a research method, to which the students should come to adhere. Instead, we assumed that each student would arrive at a unique understanding based on a combination life experiences, previous coursework and specific interactions with their instructor and peers. At the same time, we did not accept every interpretation as valid and we stressed that there are widely accepted conventions in social methodology that the students had to acknowledge. We addressed this through the concept of the 'research conversation' (see below), and more particularly by locating the emergence of particular research methods within specific social and political contexts.

The first substantive lecture in the course addressed the topic of 'controversies in social science' so as to signal that controversy is the first and most important theme in political science research methods. Following this, the different methodological traditions were presented using the notion of 'contexts of refutation' (Collini, 1983). A context of refutation is an existing approach that a new theory or approach seeks to challenge, modify or refute (Collini, 1983). Thus the course embedded the discussion of positivistic and quantitative designs and methods within a conversation about how these approaches emerged and took root in political science as part of an effort to challenge to the 'old institutionalism' (Hay, 2002, p. 11). Similarly, presentation of qualitative or interpretive designs and methods was embedded in a discussion about how these had emerged to challenge the positivistic assumption that political behaviour could be described in mechanistic, predictable terms, and asserted instead that human actors are creative, reflexive agents (Bevir, 2010; Michrina & Richards, 1996). Finally, post-structuralism was presented as a challenge to the interpretivist emphasis on 'centred' human agency, while both post-structuralism and feminist epistemologies arose to challenge the general neglect of particular kinds of power relations (Gubrium & Holstein, 2003; Law & Urry, 2004). In other words, rather than present each design or technique as simply contrasting or complementary, we sought to get students to engage with the ways that various social science research methods emerged historically as criticisms of existing approaches.

Framing methods in terms of their 'contexts of refutation' provided a space for diverse views. Some students identified strongly with the positivist critique of pre-enlightenment philosophising about politics and held to the possibility and desirability of value-free political scholarship. This allowed even the most positivistic students to argue that their approach represented a form of critical analysis. At the same time, the critique of positivist arguments produced an energizing antagonism in the class, and gave students various standpoints and vocabularies from which to expresses their frustrations with methodologies. We suspect this approach to generating engagement and dialogue was successful because the instructor avoided taking sides between the paradigms.

We also stressed the importance of contestation in course assessment, and especially the midterm exam for which students were provided in advance with a 'long list' of twenty methodological concepts and told nine concepts would be chosen from the long list to appear on the exam. In the exam they had to select six and provide a half-page written definition for each. The instructor emphasised the point that each concept was associated with a range of defensible definitions. Students were told they would be graded on the extent to which their definitions (1) represented plausible interpretations of the methodological concepts; and (2) demonstrated awareness of disagreements and debates over the definitions. Thus, the definitional exam provided students with the opportunity to highlight conceptual contestation, and reinforced the role and importance of critique in research methods.

In summary, in line with a constructivist approach we rejected the idea that students should 'learn first and question later' as impractical and inappropriate in a context where students had strongly developed critical ideas and where the majority of senior academic faculty and courses in their department also adopted critical orientations. The emphasis on contexts of refutation provided students with a clear sense that there is contestation and criticism happening within the field of methods, and gave them a means to establish their own unique position amidst the contestation.

c. Discovering empirical data and making informed choices

Our students' prior learning in political theory had primed many of them to be sceptical about empirical methods in political science. Informed by a constructivist emphasis on engaging with students' existing mental frames, the instructor sought to help students develop and refine their critiques through getting them to engage with the literature. A key student belief the instructor needed to confront was the view that only mainstream/quantitative political scientists needed to engage with issues of methodology and methods. In particular, this meant addressing their assumption that empirical methods in political science meant using statistical methods or meant being 'empiricist' – the idea that knowledge can *only* come from direct observation.

In the first few weeks the instructor helped students to refine and focus their critiques of empirical methods by introducing them to critiques of empiricism. Most moved from holding an unfocused critique of empirical work to a more specific and sophisticated critique focused on the 'problem of induction' – that is, the impossibility of making generalizations from specific cases in the absence of non-empirical assumptions (Chalmers, 1982; Hay, 2002).

Having engaged with the literature on empiricism, students were then able to distinguish between work based on an exclusively inductive approach and 'empirical' research, that is, research based *to some degree* on data collected via observation of the world. In addition, we stressed that researchers must be reflective about the historical and social context within which data collection technologies are developed and used. For example, Gubrium and Holstein's influential (2003) work on the 'interview society' was used to explore how interviewing involves a social performance with rituals, conventions and agendas, meaning interviews are not simply instruments for extracting pre-existing data from people. Finally, we engaged with the 'politics of method' (Savage & Burrows, 2007, p. 895) by introducing students to the work of Law and Urry (2004, p. 390), who argue social science methods not only enable the collection of data about social realities but also help to create or 'enact' new realities, leading to 'ontological politics', that is, to contestation and controversy about the impacts of research.

The work of Law and Urry on ontological politics was used to structure the in-class presentations and reinforce the political significance of methodological choices. Each week a group of students had to give a presentation on an article chosen by the instructor that exemplified the methods being discussed in the week's module. Students were first required to carry out a conventional methodological assessment of the articles, identifying the methods, assessing their suitability for answering the research questions, as well as determining how effectively they were implemented. In the second part of the presentation students were asked to determine what (if any) 'ontological' agendas lay behind the article and the choice of methods. The students showed great creativity in this second task. For example, one group was required to assess an article that drew on interpretive interviews with current women politicians to explore the status of 'feminism' in contemporary political discourse. The group used Weedon's aforementioned (1997) post-structuralist feminist work and Gubrium and Holstein's (2003) critique of interviewing to suggest the choice of interview methods reflected the researchers' underlying 'liberal feminist' pursuit of gender equality. In this way, students learned that knowledge of different methods is central to effective academic critique, and that choice of methods has consequences in the 'real world'.

One of the potentially negative consequences of addressing multiple methods is that a breadth of perspectives is covered at the expense of depth (Dyrhauge, 2014). The inclusion of feminist and genealogical methods alongside conventional discussions of surveys, interviews and observation leaves limited time to teach students significant skills in each area. The broad approach may conflict with the suggestion that methods instructors need to give students opportunities to carry out research (Earley, 2014). This is likely to be particularly problematic in political science where quantitative methods are dominant (Schwartz-Shea, 2003). As Kilburn et al. (2014, p. 198) argue, '[i]n the teaching of quantitative analysis the use of exercises designed to actively engage students constitute nigh on a pedagogical orthodoxy'. In the context of the honours course the shift to critical review of a range of empirical methods meant there was no longer time to devote to an in-depth examination of statistical methods.

The instructor's decision to remove the lab where students used SPSS software to run basic statistical tests generated a certain degree of consternation among some colleagues who adhered to the aforementioned orthodox view on the need for statistical exercises. The instructor chose instead to focus on 'demystifying' statistics by explaining their powers and limitations, and impressing upon students core statistical ideas such as probability sampling, significance, levels of measurement and forms of statistical validity. While this ran contrary to the quantitative orthodoxy of providing exercises, we chose the approach because it fitted with the students' needs in a context where their understandings of political science had been primarily shaped by critical theories.

Ultimately, the benefit of having multiple methods of data collection and analysis introduced in a balanced but critical way is that students get a 'taste' for several methods (Dyrhauge, 2014, p. 446); they are then in a position to make informed choices about the kinds of methods they want to pursue in the future – how they want to construct their long term learning on the subject. In this sense we took seriously the course mandate to provide an introduction to research methods rather than to focus on slightly more advanced techniques in a narrow area.

d. *Research as a conversation*

One of the risks of presenting methods as contested and political is that students develop a nihilistic and cynical view of methodologies as artificial and arbitrary categories whose only or primary functions are to police knowledge, maintain the hegemony of the 'official truth', and prevent new 'subaltern knowledges' from being promoted. A review of the first author's diary from the first year revealed that some students reacted in precisely this manner. For example, one journal entry mentions an email exchange with a student frustrated about the range of research designs and methodologies presented in the course. The student argues their preferred research does not fit neatly into the research designs outlined. The student claims these categories exemplify Foucault's description of disciplinary power: they force students to adapt their research interests to existing analytical schemas, and to measure their work against standards imposed by others. The student asserts they are not alone in the class in feeling such frustrations. The instructor's response to this was to complement the focus on contestation with a discussion of the *research conversation*.

The existing methods literature has promoted the concept of the 'research conversation' as a metaphor for how scholars should frame and communicate their research findings (Booth, Colomb, & Williams, 2003; Denzin, 2009). The idea is that research should contribute to an ongoing dialogue, in which people have shared interests but different perspectives. The metaphor usefully conveys the notion that a researcher should not attempt to speak over others, stop the conversation or abruptly change the topic. Most importantly for our students worried about being boxed in by categories, the conversation metaphor highlights the importance of having a shared vocabulary in order to efficiently convey one's scholarly intensions and actions (Booth et al., 2003). In this approach, methodological concepts and standard research designs are not prison cells, but signalling devices that allow the researcher to quickly convey to others her mode of operation.

To operationalize this idea, the instructor routinely required students to summarise their research before the whole class in restricted time, using the same idea as the 'three minute thesis' competition (http://threeminutethesis.org/, 2014). Students were also required to describe their research to a peer, who in turn had to relay the project to the whole class. In addition, the in-class presentations were deliberately allocated restricted time to encourage students to be succinct in describing and assessing the authors' methods. Putting students under pressure to describe their own and others' research in concise form reinforced the benefit of a common methodological vocabulary.

In the second delivery of the course the instructor stressed that these categories and concepts were starting points from which one could build in modifications, and that having a shared vocabulary helped researchers to identify and clarify the uniqueness of their contributions relative to established practice. Finally, the course stressed that there is not one but multiple research conversations. Each conversation possesses its own vernacular but is, nevertheless, shaped by the more generic methodological concepts that have cross-disciplinary currency. The existence of multiple conversations allowed the instructor to push responsibility back to the students who objected to being boxed in, by challenging them: *If you don't like my categories, tell me who you want to have a research conversation with, and what concepts and categories they use.*

Discussion

In this paper we have sought to present strategies for teaching research methods after the critical turn. The pedagogical challenge was to overcome scepticism and hostility towards empirical analysis and demonstrate the validity and importance of primary research. While our case study addressed a political science department with an unusually critical orientation, our findings have broader significance for methods teaching in the social sciences. We now address the implications of our case study for two key teaching challenges: the integration of methods into the substantive curriculum, and the need for methods training to foster critical skills.

Several reviews of political science methods courses at Anglo-American universities have criticised the lack of integration of methods into the broader curriculum. In these countries methods tend to be taught in stand-alone courses. One solution proposed by these authors (see, e.g. Leston-Bandeira, 2013; Parker, 2010) is to spread discussion of methods out to other courses. While we support this idea in principle, our case study suggests that integration can also occur in the reverse direction: that is, we can bring more of the substantive curriculum into methods courses by presenting methods in the context of larger disciplinary debates. To achieve this, those who design and deliver methods courses need to give greater consideration to their departmental and disciplinary context. Through reflection, on-going conversations about our respective methods teaching experiences, and our systematic review of the literature, we have come to hold that current textbooks and the current literature pay inadequate attention to the role that the departmental and disciplinary context plays in how students engage with and interpret courses in social research methods. The constructivist emphasis on uncovering individual, departmental and disciplinary contexts provides the basis for better connections between substantive degree content and methodological training.

Researchers have also highlighted the absence of critical approaches in social research methods teaching. Many political science methods courses continue to employ outmoded transmission models. In our case study there was no shortage of critical thinking among the methods students. However, our students initially approached methods with an unfocused critique of positivistic reasoning, with little understanding of the nuanced distinctions within and between quantitative and qualitative methodologies. They were joined by other students who desired more conventional methods training. Our experience suggests constructivist pedagogy allows methods instructors to both adapt to the intellectual context and respond to learners with diverse needs and interests. In particular, the concept of 'contexts of refutation' has been especially useful in highlighting the many different forms of legitimate methodological critique and their role in driving methodological innovation. Furthermore, the notion of the 'research conversation' encourages students to express their critiques in ways that engage and advance existing debates.

The first author has since adapted these principles to teaching masters students in a professional public administration program, while the second author has used them to teach coursework masters students in development and community relations. These students are usually working as public servants, on-the-ground development officers, or in community relations in the mining industry, and have had minimal exposure to the critical turn. Yet they identify with our constructivist strategies and concepts. One public administration student commented that the context of refutation reminded her of the constant efforts by governments to discredit their predecessors' policies. Another suggested the research conversation is also vital in government, because research carried out by the public service has no impact unless staff can engage and persuade decision makers. Thus, we are confident these constructivist strategies are applicable and useful across a variety of different methods courses – not just those taken by students immersed in post-structuralism. We hope our experiences and reflections provide beneficial ideas for our fellow methods instructors.

Disclosure statement

No potential conflict of interest was reported by the authors.

Note

1. We determined this via a review of the syllabi for undergraduate methods courses offered in the top 20 political science departments in the world, as well as the top 10 in Canada, according to the QS World Rankings in 2014 (http://www.topuniversities.com/courses/politics/guide).

References

Bacchi, C. L. (2009). *Analysing policy: What's the problem represented to be?* Sydney: Pearson Education.
Bang, H. P., & Esmark, A. (2007). *New publics with/out democracy*. Frederiksberg: Samfundslitteratur.
Bevir, M. (2010). *The sage handbook of governance*. London: Sage.
Blalock, Jr., H. M. (1987). Some general goals in teaching statistics. *Teaching Sociology, 15*, 164–172.
Booth, W. C., Colomb, G. G., & Williams, J. M. (2003). *The craft of research* (2nd ed.). Chicago, IL: University of Chicago Press.
Bridges, G. S., Gillmore, G. M., Pershing, J. L., & Bates, K. A. (1998). Teaching quantitative research methods: A quasi-experimental analysis. *Teaching Sociology, 26*, 14–28.
Burawoy, M. (2005). The critical turn to public sociology. *Critical Sociology, 31*, 313–326.
Chalmers, A. (1982). *What is this thing called science?* St. Lucia: University of Queensland.
Collini, S. (1983). *Liberalism and sociology: LT hobhouse and political argument in England 1880–1914*. Cambridge: Cambridge University Press.
Denzin, N. K. (2009). The elephant in the living room: Or extending the conversation about the politics of evidence. *Qualitative Research, 9*, 139–160.
Dyrhauge, H. (2014). Teaching qualitative methods in social science: A problem-based learning approach. *Journal of Contemporary European Research, 10*, 442–455.
Earley, M. A. (2014). A synthesis of the literature on research methods education. *Teaching in Higher Education, 19*, 242–253.
Fischer, F. (2009). *Democracy and expertise*. Oxford: Oxford University Press.
Gubrium, J. F., & Holstein, J. A. (2003). *Postmodern interviewing*. Thousand Oaks, CA: Sage.
Hajer, M. (2003). Policy without polity? Policy analysis and the institutional void. *Policy Sciences, 36*, 175–195.
Hammersley, M. (2005). Should social science be critical? *Philosophy of the Social Sciences, 35*, 175–195.
Hawker, J., McMillan, A., & Palermo, C. (2013). Enduring mentoring partnership: A reflective case study and recommendations for evaluating mentoring in dietetics. *Nutrition & Dietetics, 70*, 339–344.
Hay, C. (2002). *Political analysis: A critical introduction*. Basingstoke: Palgrave Macmillan.
Kilburn, D., Nind, M., & Wiles, R. (2014). Learning as researchers and teachers: The development of a pedagogical culture for social science research methods? *British Journal of Educational Studies, 62*, 191–207.
Law, J., & Urry, J. (2004). Enacting the social. *Economy and Society, 33*, 390–410.
Leston-Bandeira, C. (2013). Methods teaching through a discipline research-oriented approach. *Politics, 33*, 207–219.
Lloyd, M., & Thacker, A. (1997). *The impact of Michel Foucault on the social sciences and humanities*. New York, NY: St Martin's Press.
Marfleet, B. G., & Dille, B. J. (2005). Information literacy and the undergraduate research methods curriculum. *Journal of Political Science Education, 1*, 175–190.
Marsh, D., & Stoker, G. (2002). *Theories and methods in political science*. Basingstoke: Palgrave Macmillan.
Michrina, B. P., & Richards, C. (1996). *Person to person: Fieldwork, dialogue, and the hermeneutic method*. Albany, NY: SUNY Press.
Navarro, V. (2005). Constructing a teacher of qualitative methods: A reflection. *International Journal of Social Research Methodology, 8*, 419–435.
Oldland, E. (2011). Transition from clinical manager to university lecturer: A self-reflective case study. *Higher Education Research & Development, 30*, 779–790.
Parker, J. (2010). Undergraduate research-methods training in political science: A comparative perspective. *PS: Political Science & Politics, 43*, 121–125.
Richardson, V. (2003). Constructivist pedagogy. *Teachers College Record, 105*, 1623–1640.
Ryan, M., Saunders, C., Rainsford, E., & Thompson, E. (2014). Improving research methods teaching and learning in politics and international relations: A 'reality show' approach. *Politics, 34*, 85–97.

Savage, M., & Burrows, R. (2007). The coming crisis of empirical sociology. *Sociology, 41*, 885–899.

Schmidt, V. A. (2008). Discursive institutionalism: The explanatory power of ideas and discourse. *Annual Review of Political Science, 11*, 303–326.

Schwartz-Shea, P. (2003). Is this the curriculum we want? Doctoral requirements and offerings in methods and methodology. *Political Science and Politics, 36*, 379–386.

Scott, L. (2014). "Digging deep": Self-study as a reflexive approach to improving my practice as an artist, researcher and teacher. *Perspectives in Education: Self-Study of Educational Practice: Re-Imagining our Pedagogies, 32*, 69–88.

Spigner-Littles, D. A., & Chalon, E. (1999). Constructivism: A paradigm for older learners. *Educational Gerontology, 25*, 203–209.

Tenenbaum, G., Naidu, S., Jegede, O., & Austin, J. (2001). Constructivist pedagogy in conventional on-campus and distance learning practice: An exploratory investigation. *Learning and Instruction, 11*, 87–111.

Wagner, C., Garner, M., & Kawulich, B. (2011). The state of the art of teaching research methods in the social sciences: Towards a pedagogical culture. *Studies in Higher Education, 36*, 75–88.

Weedon, C. (1997). *Feminist practice and poststructuralist theory* (2nd ed.). Victoria: Blackwell.

Yan, H. (2013). Constructive learning and the design of a tourism postgraduate research methods module. *Journal of Teaching in Travel & Tourism, 13*, 52–74.

Yanow, D., & Schwartz-Shea, P. (2013). *Interpretation and method: Empirical research methods and the interpretive turn.* New York, NY: ME Sharpe.

From guided-instruction to facilitation of learning: the development of *Five-level QDA* as a CAQDAS pedagogy that explicates the practices of expert users

Christina Silver[a] and Nicholas H. Woolf[b]

[a]*Qualitative Data Analysis Services, Dorset, UK;* [b]*Woolf Consulting Inc, Santa Barbara, CA, USA*

> This paper introduces *Five-level QDA* (Qualitative Data Analysis) as a pedagogy for the teaching and learning of CAQDAS (Computer Assisted Qualitative Data AnalysiS) that spans methodologies, software packages and teaching modes. Based on the authors' personal trajectories of using, teaching and researching CAQDAS since the late-1990s, the paper illustrates the need for a CAQDAS pedagogy by describing the challenges of learners in powerfully harnessing CAQDAS packages. The principles behind *Five-level QDA* are outlined, which focus on the contrast between the strategies and tactics of conducting QDA with software, and the need to translate between these. The implementation of *Five-level QDA* as an adaptable method of instruction is illustrated through the use of *Analytic Planning Worksheets* in the *Recurring Hourglass* design.

Introduction

Computer Assisted Qualitative Data AnalysiS (CAQDAS) packages have been available since the 1980s, yet despite extensive use and the work of several authors that address the challenges of teaching CAQDAS (di Gregorio & Davidson, 2008; Lewins & Silver, 2007; Silver & Lewins, 2014), no general pedagogy has been developed that is applicable across methodologies, software packages, and teaching modes. The absence of widespread embedding of CAQDAS instruction into university curricular (Silver & Rivers, 2014) reflects the broader marginalised position occupied by the teaching of research techniques and methodologies (Kilburn, Nind, & Wiles, 2014). However, the plethora of digital tools available to support research work (Paulus, Lester, & Dempster, 2014) means researchers increasingly expect to employ customized software to undertake analysis. Teachers are therefore responsible for developing appropriate and effective pedagogies that take account of variety in research methodologies and analytic techniques and that equip learners with the skills required to undertake robust computer-assisted analyses.

Learning CAQDAS happens in many ways. Workshop-based training for groups is the most common, offered in many formats by different providers. Various online resources are also provided by software developers, university teachers and independent consultants, including video tutorials, user manuals, analytically-oriented support materials, online courses, remote coaching options (di Gregorio, 2014; Kaczynski & Kelly, 2004), and a small but increasing number of modules at Higher Education Institutions (Davis & Krayer, 2014; Gibbs, 2014). The range of learning options is testament to both the variety in individual learning styles (Honey & Mumford, 1982) and the ongoing demand for CAQDAS teaching. Rapid CAQDAS software development and increasing use across sectors, disciplines and methodologies compounds the need to develop a CAQDAS pedagogy that transcends the specificities of products, methodological applications and modes of teaching.

This paper presents a CAQDAS pedagogy that meets these criteria and that is incorporated into our teaching practices. We first outline how our individual trajectories of using and teaching CAQDAS packages led us to identify the nature of researchers' struggles to employ CAQDAS packages powerfully, and thus the requirements of a general CAQDAS pedagogy. Using CAQDAS packages powerfully means using a program from the start to finish of a project while remaining true throughout to the emergent ethos of qualitative data analysis (QDA). In each of our trajectories we moved from an initial focus on guided-instruction to an increasing emphasis on facilitated learning in order to overcome the challenges of learning to use CAQDAS programs powerfully. However, whilst independently arriving at common principles, our emphasis was different. Silver focused on challenges caused by diversity amongst CAQDAS packages, varieties in their users and uses, and curriculum design of workshops as her predominant mode of instruction. Her key outcome was the *Recurring Hourglass* workshop design which enables learners to acquire abstract knowledge and practical experience by alternating learning activities and instructional methods. Woolf focused on learners' challenges in moving beyond straightforward to sophisticated uses of CAQDAS, and the need to unpack the 'black–box' of expert use that develops over many years of practice. His key outcome was a model of the CAQDAS process that expert users may undertake unconsciously, focusing on the contrasts between the strategies and tactics of a QDA when conducted with software, and the need to translate between them (Woolf, 2014). Since meeting in 2013, we have collaborated to develop and implement an adaptable CAQDAS pedagogy based on two innovations, referred to as *Five-level QDA*, which is designed to facilitate the learning of sophisticated uses of CAQDAS packages. In this paper we illustrate the implementation of *Five-level QDA* in the context of intensive two-day CAQDAS workshops using Analytic Planning Worksheets embedded within the *Recurring Hourglass* design.

Silver's personal trajectory and the evolution of the *Recurring Hourglass* design
Phase 1: guided-instruction (ca. 1997–2002)
My experience during postgraduate research as a concurrent learner-teacher, with frequent delivery of intensive workshop-based training via my role at the CAQDAS Networking Project (CNP),[1] served as a gradual enculturation into a community of practice of CAQDAS teachers (Lave & Wenger, 1991). CAQDAS use was not yet widespread and experienced researchers were primarily interested in learning what these new technologies 'could do', seeking streamlined ways of undertaking already established analytic practices. Many had limited experience with complex computer packages and required step-by-step instruction in software operation. These factors informed workshop delivery via *guided-instruction* in the operation of the software.

Hand-outs containing detailed step-by-step instructions in software operation were refined and expanded as new software versions became available and were increasingly embedded as both an in-workshop learning tool and post-workshop resource.

The pedagogic aims of this whole-group hands-on experience were to familiarize learners with CAQDAS functionality by performing analytic tasks using sample data, and to encourage them to reflect on its potential role for their own projects. Such experiential learning involving concrete experience, observation and experimentation (Kolb, 1984) is a feature of my training provision throughout my trajectory.

During this phase, the standard one-day workshops followed a structured plan designed to impart key facts and to encourage learners' to employ features creatively for their own needs. Although the workshops succeeded in imparting the necessary information to operate software and were positively evaluated, it became clear that the focus and delivery were insufficiently flexible to accommodate a growing range of learner needs. As interest in and uptake of CAQDAS increased so did learner heterogeneity, and the need became increasingly pressing to deliver workshops that were more responsive to participants' varied needs. Additionally, teaching many CAQDAS packages highlighted their differences and the recognition that there is no 'best' CAQDAS package or ideal way of using the programs. Rather, they need to be chosen and used according to individual project characteristics (Fielding & Lee, 1991). This led to a transition to instruction-led facilitation in which the importance of planning for software use was prioritized.

Phase 2: instruction-led facilitation (ca. 2002–2008)

New CAQDAS packages and an increase in demand for training and on-going support led to more bespoke in-house workshops and personal coaching for researchers and project teams. To better meet learners' increasingly diverse needs, intensive one-day introductory workshops were redesigned to emphasize different uses of software. *Guided-instruction* using sample data was augmented with project-based illustrations from my own research and the use of learners' projects as instructional examples. Technical instruction concerning the logic and functioning of software remained core, but emphasis shifted towards facilitating the use of software features for the analytic needs of learners' own projects, and reflecting on the implications arising from illustration of my own projects. This allowed time for learners to experiment with software independently. Additionally, advanced workshops and user seminars were provided by the CNP to meet the needs of cohorts of existing CAQDAS users. Learners brought their work-in-progress and time was allotted to sharing and reflecting on the successes and challenges of using software for specific research projects.

An outcome of this phase was the first edition of *Using Software in Qualitative Research: A Step-by-step Guide* (Lewins & Silver, 2007), a textbook which included a model of common QDA processes: *integrating data, exploring data, identifying and organizing data, asking questions* and *interpretation*. Framing workshop instruction around these processes using real-world examples allowed the potential role and flexibility of CAQDAS packages to be more concretely illustrated. This transition to *instruction-led facilitation* was positively evaluated, and this emphasis on the agency of learners developed further during phase three.

The model of common QDA processes for planning software use in the context of specific project needs (Lewins & Silver, 2007) was a step forward in communicating the potential role of CAQDAS packages. Other textbooks and training providers have also related software features to analytic processes with their own standard models of underlying QDA processes (e.g. di Gregorio & Davidson, 2008; Friese, 2014). However, this approach is problematic because it can be misconstrued as a 'one-size-fits-all' model, which risks propagating the perception that software is a method rather than a tool. An outcome of increasing learners' agency in workshops during the second phase was feedback that learners would benefit from illustrations that were more explicitly methodological. These observations led to further developments in textbook content and workshop delivery.

Phase 3: facilitation-led instruction (ca. 2008–2013)

In order to address these issues the CNP undertook qualitative longitudinal research tracking researchers' learning and use of CAQDAS packages over 12 months (Silver, 2010). Results illustrated that successful use was related to methodological awareness, adeptness in the techniques of analysis, and technological proficiency (Silver & Rivers, 2014). *Methodological awareness* refers to familiarity with the variety in QDA philosophies and methodological approaches that underpin the choices researchers make in undertaking analysis. *Analytic adeptness* concerns learners' experience in undertaking QDA, specifically the skills in designing analytic tasks in the context of underlying methodology and philosophy. *Technological proficiency* refers to competency in operating software and comfort with the idea of experimentation without fear of making mistakes. These findings informed the second edition of the textbook to incorporate a case-study approach (Silver & Lewins, 2014), and the re-focusing of workshop delivery to become more specific to the varied methodological contexts and analytic activities of each learner. The pedagogy that evolved constituted an intentional shift towards *facilitation-led instruction* by further emphasizing the responsibility of learners to plan in detail for their own software use in the context of their own methodologies, and culminated in the development of the *Recurring Hourglass* workshop design (Figure 1).

It was not feasible to provide examples of software use for the full range of qualitative methodologies. Instead case-studies were developed to illustrate the potential of CAQDAS in supporting each aspect of the research process, from problem formulation and literature review through data analysis to final write-up, without prescribing a 'one-size-fits-all' method for any methodological approach or analytic task. This was achieved by contrasting the *commonalities* in analytic activities across methodologies, and the *differences* in how they manifest in the selection and use of software features for specific analytic needs. The model from the 2007 textbook was thus adapted to focus on the analytic activities of *integration, organisation, reflection, exploration* and *interrogation* (2014, p. 45), and discussed both in terms of the case-studies and learners' own projects, to facilitate them in designing appropriate ways of using CAQDAS features.

Additional instructional strategies were required to implement this expanded workshop instruction, culminating in the *Recurring Hourglass* design (see Figure 1). This is an adaptation of the elaboration theory of instruction (Reigeluth, 1979), and is designed to be applicable to face-to-face workshops of varying lengths and formats.

THE TEACHING AND LEARNING OF SOCIAL RESEARCH METHODS

Focus ===== Level of learning	Instructional design
DAY 1	
Narrow ===== Whole-group	*OBJECTIVE:* INTRODUCTIONS • Set the tone of the workshop and establish a conducive learning environment via teacher and learner introductions. • Identify similarities and differences in participants' projects to foster connections and prompt discussion. INSTRUCTIONAL STRATEGIES • Describe research experience and background, current project, needs from and expectations of training.
Broad ===== Whole-group	*OBJECTIVE:* CONTEXTUAL DISCUSSIONS • Ensure learning is grounded in appropriate contexts • Emphasize the flexibility and adaptability of software, thereby encouraging learners to reflect on their specific needs and to carefully plan for their use of software. • Establish the agency of learners in workshop-based learning and in appropriately manipulating software features INSTRUCTIONAL STRATEGIES • Slide-illustrated lecture discussing relevant underlying contexts: developmental; methodological; analytic; and practical and analytic activities: integration, organization, exploration, reflection and interrogation (drawn from Silver & Lewins, 2014). • Introduce *Five-level QDA* as a means of distinguishing between analytic strategies and tactics
Broad ===== Whole-group	*OBJECTIVE:* SOFTWARE OVERVIEW • Introduce software in its entirety to raise awareness of the breadth of its application and potential affordances to learners' work INSTRUCTIONAL STRATEGIES • High-level description and illustration of software architecture and features via guided walk-through using a sample project
Narrow = Individual ====	*OBJECTIVE:* ANALYTIC PLANNING #1 • Introduce Analytic Planning Worksheets (APWs) (Figure 3) as a tool for effectively designing software-assisted analysis INSTRUCTIONAL STRATEGIES • Illustration of partially completed Analytic Planning Worksheet and discussion about its logic in relation to project characteristics • Provide learners' with time to begin completing an APW for Levels 1 & 2 (objectives and general analytic plan)
Narrow ===== Whole-group	*OBJECTIVE:* GUIDED-INSTRUCTION • Provide opportunity for hands-on experimentation of straightforward uses of software features in the context of a real-world project INSTRUCTIONAL STRATEGIES • Step-by-step guided set-up of a software project following the APW illustrated in Analytic Planning #1 workshop phase
Broad ===== Whole-group	*OBJECTIVE:* ILLUSTRATIVE DISCUSSIONS • Illustrate range of applications of software features • Ensure examples are relevant to learners' contexts • Encourage reflection on the affordances of software features for learners' particular needs INSTRUCTIONAL STRATEGIES • Demonstration and discussion of several contrasting software projects to illustrate the influence of project characteristics on use of software • Illustrations related to contextual discussions and learners' projects

Figure 1. The *Recurring Hourglass* design: example of a two-day model with embedded *Five-level QDA*.

It is intended to build knowledge cumulatively such that each stage of instruction serves to elaborate the previous stage as well as serving as an overview of the next stage of elaboration.

Narrow ===== Individual	*OBJECTIVE:* INDEPENDENT APPLICATION • Provide learners with opportunity to begin applying learning in the context of their own project needs INSTRUCTIONAL STRATEGIES • Learners create new software project and set it up for their specific needs • Learners are supported as required with specifics of software operation
DAY 2	
Narrow ===== Whole- group	*OBJECTIVE:* LEARNER SUMMARIES • Encourage reflection on the learning from day one, focus attention on objectives for day two and re-establish focus of workshop INSTRUCTIONAL STRATEGIES • Describe ways in which it is envisaged software will be used. Outline intentions for the day
Narrow ===== Individual	*OBJECTIVE:* ANALYTIC PLANNING #2 • Revisit APW and with key learning objectives for the day in mind fill out Levels 1, 2a and 2b in as much detail as possible INSTRUCTIONAL STRATEGIES • Short review of partially completed APW serves as a reminder of the logic of the Worksheet and its role in planning for powerful software use. • Facilitator supports individual learners fill out APW as required
Narrow ===== Individual	*OBJECTIVE:* INDEPENDENT APPLICATION • Learners continue with own work, following their APW INSTRUCTIONAL STRATEGIES • Facilitator spends time with each learner providing individual coaching as required • If several learners are struggling with operating software for a similar analytic task, individual work is interrupted to instruct the group as a whole
Broad ===== Whole- group	*OBJECTIVE:* ILLUSTRATIVE DISCUSSIONS • Illustrate a selection of sophisticated uses of software tools in real-world research projects • Enable learners to reflect on the implications of contextual discussions, refine analytic planning and translate abstract learning to their own needs INSTRUCTIONAL STRATEGIES • Demonstration and discussion of several contrasting software projects to illustrate the influence of project characteristics on use of software • Illustrations related to contextual discussions and participants' projects
Narrow ===== Individual	*OBJECTIVE:* INDEPENDENT APPLICATION • Participants continue with own work, following their APW INSTRUCTIONAL STRATEGIES • Facilitator spends time with each participant providing individual coaching as required • If several participants are struggling with operating software for a similar analytic task, individual work is interrupted to instruct the group as a whole
Narrow ===== Individual	*OBJECTIVE:* ANALYTIC PLANNING #3 • Revisit APW, focusing on Levels 3, 4 and 5 • Introduce Translation Worksheets and show how to fill one out INSTRUCTIONAL STRATEGIES • Description of the process of translation and the difference between selecting and constructing tools • Illustrate that different tools may be used to fulfil the same set of analytic tasks and that appropriate choices are determined by methodology and principles guiding QDA and the general analytic plan
Broad ===== Whole- group	*OBJECTIVE:* ILLUSTRATIVE DISCUSSIONS • Illustrate a selection of sophisticated uses of software tools in real-world research projects • Enable participants to reflect on the implications of contextual discussions, refine analytic planning and translate abstract learning to their own needs INSTRUCTIONAL STRATEGIES • Demonstration and discussion of several contrasting software projects to illustrate the influence of project characteristics on use of software • Illustrations related to contextual discussions and participants' projects
Broad	*OBJECTIVE:* CONTEXTUAL DISCUSSIONS

Figure 1. (*Continued*).

===== Whole- group	• Remind participants of contexts within which software is used and range of analytic activities that can be undertaken using software • Provide opportunity for participants to discuss their work INSTRUCTIONAL STRATEGIES • Revisit contextual discussion slides used on day one to frame discussion • Q&A in relation to participant projects
Broad ===== Whole- group	*OBJECTIVE:* PREPARATION FOR POST-WORKSHOP • Prepare participants for post-workshop software use INSTRUCTIONAL STRATEGIES • Review range of resources available • Demonstrate how to access online materials • List sources of individual support
Narrow ===== Whole- group	*OBJECTIVE:* PARTICIPANT REFLECTIONS Encourage participants to reflect on learning and plan for continued software use. INSTRUCTIONAL STRATEGIES Summarise individual key learning outcomes and planned next steps with analysis

Figure 1. (*Continued*).

The design alternates activities with a broad, whole-group focus and a narrow, individual focus, hence the term *Recurring Hourglass* for this repeated oscillation between foci, and is based on an important lesson of the prior two phases: learning how to effectively use CAQDAS features requires a comprehensive understanding of the role, functioning and potential of CAQDAS packages *before* learning how to operate the software. This preliminary understanding is referred to by Reigeluth (1979) as the top-level *epitome*, or conceptual orientation to the coming material that is presented at an application level without requiring learning pre-requisites. In CAQDAS workshops this includes an overview of the software as a whole, illustration of its longer-term potential in later phases of a data analysis, and the appropriate use of software features in different phases of a data analysis. The complexity of CAQDAS packages and the diversity of learners' prior experience and current needs requires careful management in order to balance the acquisition of abstract knowledge and practical hands-on experience.

Alternating workshop activities occur in different sequences and frequencies depending on workshop format, learner needs, and the momentum and progress of individual workshops, enabling methodologically relevant facilitation of learning, which involves illustrating uses of software tools in a variety of analytic contexts. Figure 1 illustrates in detail the instructional strategies in a typical two-day workshop using the design.

The generally accepted criteria for successful instructional design is that students find instruction efficient, appealing, and effective (Smith & Ragan, 2005). The pedagogy in this phase was more successful in the first two criteria than the third. Participant feedback indicated that the use of real-world examples and a variety of instructional strategies were indeed efficient and appealing ways to make the teaching of CAQDAS packages more relevant to their needs. However, while the focus on analytic activities, the case study approach, and the *Recurring Hourglass* design emphasized user agency in using software features appropriately; research (Silver & Rivers, 2014), observation of learners, and participant feedback suggest that learners still struggle to employ CAQDAS powerfully in their own work after the workshop. Enabling learners to translate workshop illustrations into their own practice is the core issue of the collaboration between both authors to implement *Five-level QDA* as a CAQDAS pedagogy applicable across methodologies, software packages and teaching modes.

Woolf's personal trajectory and the evolution of the framework for *Five-level QDA*

Phase 1: guided-instruction (ca. 1997–2003)

While conducting postgraduate research in the early 1990's I concluded that to develop sufficient CAQDAS expertise I needed to select a single package that could be adapted to the widest range of methodologies. I chose ATLAS.ti, and after using the program in a number of projects and coaching other students and instructors in the software, I taught a post-graduate class at the University of Iowa in CAQDAS, devoting one quarter of each class to instruction in operating ATLAS.ti. I began conducting two-day workshops across the USA with the same focus on teaching the operation of the software features in a logical order that matched the kinds of research projects I was involved in, typically using grounded theory approaches and content analysis.

Many participants requested post-workshop coaching, an experience that highlighted two limitations of this *guided-instruction* pedagogy. First, many learners were not conducting grounded theory or content analysis, and had either set up their projects as if they were or were using the software only for data management or initial coding. Others had a different problem: instruction in software operation out of the context of their own studies led to inert knowledge, knowledge gained out of the context of a real application and that is not later used in problem solving even though relevant (Whitehead, 1929). During follow-up consultations learners had to be instructed afresh in the selection and use of software features appropriate for their data analyses. These observations led me to adopt an anchored-instruction approach in the second phase, in which the software could be perceived as a tool for problem-solving as an expert would use it, rather than an arbitrary procedure (Bransford, Sherwood, Hasselbring, Kinzer, & Williams, 1990). Rather than teaching software features independent of a specific use, I adopted an *instruction-led facilitation* approach in order to enable learners' to problem-solve in their own projects.

Phase 2: instruction-led facilitation (ca. 2003–2010)

To avoid the problem of inert knowledge described above, I identified three key learning objectives for gaining transferable CAQDAS skills in workshop contexts: (i) to understand the software architecture as a whole through a conceptual overview of the entire program, to serve as an extended *advance organizer* (see below); (ii) to learn to conceptually harness the software for the particular purposes of a variety of studies; and finally (iii) to learn to operate the software features and put the first two objectives into practice.

Initially I alternated instruction amongst these three learning tasks in small chunks of one to two hours each. Over time the critical importance of the *advance organizer*, and the lowest priority of learning to operate the software features, became more and more apparent, based on learners' feedback during the workshops and their ability to later employ the software successfully. An advance organizer is the 'introduction of relevant subsuming concepts' prior to learning unfamiliar material (Ausubel & Robinson, 1969, p. 29). Mayer (1979) reported that in the case of 'expository advance organizers', such as my extended conceptual overviews of the architecture of the software, the advance organizer has its strongest effect on the later transfer of knowledge to new domains (p. 382). In accordance with these principles, the extended conceptual overview was presented in complete form at the outset, and often filled the entire first day of the workshop without participants opening their laptops until the second day. This workshop design was evaluated more positively by participants.

Despite the advantages of this workshop design it was still apparent that participants experienced difficulty in transferring their learning to using the software powerfully in their own projects. Silver, who experienced the same phenomenon at approximately the same time in the UK, addressed this by developing the *Recurring Hourglass* design. I approached the issue differently by addressing the need to further unpack the process of powerfully harnessing software that develops in CAQDAS experts over time.

Phase 3: facilitation-led instruction (ca. 2010–2013)

The third phase was characterized by unpacking CAQDAS experts' processes for harnessing CAQDAS packages, such that learners could more quickly employ software powerfully. Observation of my own research practices, the practices of other long-time researchers, and the challenges of novice researchers, led to the recognition that CAQDAS expertise lies in effectively reconciling the underlying contradiction between the strategies and tactics of a QDA when conducted with software. The strategies – *what you plan to do* –are to varying degrees iterative and emergent, while the tactics – *how you plan to do it* –comprise the use of cut-and-dried, pre-determined computer software tools. Novices often approach the process by first learning the software operations and looking for ways of using them in the data analysis, not recognizing the underlying contradiction or the need to reconcile it. Experts learn over time that powerful CAQDAS use begins by first specifying analytic tasks without regard to the available program features, and then harnessing appropriate software tools to accomplish the tasks.

The second learning objective – learning to conceptually harness the software for particular purposes in each learners' study – was therefore reoriented to distinguish strategies from tactics in a QDA and demonstrate the process of translating between them. However, while learners appreciated the value of this process in the context of specific illustrations, they could not reliably transfer the learning to their own, novel situations after the workshop. It became clear that the translation process was not sufficiently explicated as a systematic process. I therefore searched the literature for a model of strategy and tactics that could inform the CAQDAS process.

Military studies is amongst few disciplines that investigate this relationship between strategies and tactics. The military strategist Edward Luttwak (2001) identified five levels of strategy as a descriptive model that does not prescribe specific courses of action, but provides the principles applicable to any context of conflict. At first glance a military metaphor does not appear apposite to qualitative research. Yet Luttwak's five levels bear an uncanny resemblance to the general processes applicable to the use of CAQDAS packages regardless of the specifics of the methodology or the content of a project, just as Luttwak's model describes the general processes of military strategy regardless of the type of conflict. Luttwak (2001)'s seminal contribution, now incorporated into army training manuals, is the identification of a middle level of operational coordination between strategies and tactics that is itself neither a strategy nor a tactic, but serves as the fulcrum between them. The characteristics of this middle level of operational coordination in the military context correspond closely to the middle level of translation between the strategies and tactics of a QDA that is undertaken unconsciously by expert CAQDAS users. Luttwak's (2001) exposition of military strategy informed the formalization of the expert process of CAQDAS as *Five-level QDA* (Woolf, 2014).

Learners' struggles to harness CAQDAS powerfully and the principles underlying *Five-level QDA*

Our separate experiences of teaching thousands of researchers and students, observing and investigating how they learn and use CAQDAS packages, and undertaking and consulting on numerous software-assisted analyses, has resulted in our continual reflection about the most effective ways to equip users with the skills required to harness CAQDAS packages powerfully. We independently reached the same conclusion: that learning how to use CAQDAS effectively requires a comprehensive overview of software architecture, a sense of its longer-term potential and the appropriate use of individual features at different stages of a project; *before* learning to operate any aspect of the software. We each gradually modified our workshop designs to give primacy to learning to harness rather than simply operate software, and to alternate these learning tasks. Despite our different backgrounds and teaching contexts, our observations of learners' struggles and our approaches to enabling them to overcome these are similar. Three principle causes of learners' struggles to use software powerfully underlie our refinement and implementation of *Five-level QDA*.

First is the misconception that there is an ideal or right way to use CAQDAS packages. The one-size-fits-all models often presented in textbooks are inappropriate because the objectives, methodologies, and analytic procedures of individual projects are so varied. It is neither possible nor appropriate to teach CAQDAS as if it were a uniform method.

Second is the skill of harnessing software features for sophisticated uses. Learning CAQDAS packages in a mechanical way, by focussing on operating the software out of the context of accomplishing particular analytic tasks, may be sufficient to allow researchers to use the software effectively for straightforward purposes. But CAQDAS users must often go beyond straightforward uses by harnessing software features in combined or unusual ways for more sophisticated uses that may not have been anticipated by the software developer, and may not be apparent from the presentation of the features on the computer screen.

Finally, the methods literature speaks almost exclusively of iterative and emergent analytic strategies, without distinguishing the contrasting characteristics of the more cut-and-dried tactics that will be used to execute those strategies, whether the tactics are coloured markers and whiteboards or CAQDAS packages. In the case of CAQDAS packages, thinking of analytic strategies and software tactics as a single activity can increase the challenge of going beyond straightforward uses of the software. This is compounded when the analytic strategy is not sufficiently clear, and the software features are used as a kind of substitute for steps of analysis, making the analysis less iterative and emergent than is appropriate.

These principles frame our work in combining the most effective elements of each of our practices into an explicit method of teaching and using CAQDAS packages: *Five-level QDA,* a process that enables learners to harness software features to the needs of a specific analytic task as the last step of the analytic process, as opposed to first instructing them in mechanical software operations which then drive the choice and design of the analytic tasks that are undertaken.

Five-level QDA *and translation*

When CAQDAS packages are used in a mechanical way, use is often restricted to early project phases, or features are used in a more mechanical manner than is called for by the methodology. Powerful use refers to using CAQDAS packages for every stage of a project, from the very start to the very end, while remaining true throughout to the iterative and emergent spirit of qualitative research. This involves harnessing software features rather than simply operating them, and is achieved by distinguishing analytic strategies (which are to varying degrees iterative and emergent) from analytic tactics (which in the case of using computer software are more cut-and-dried) and consciously translating between them. This process, which we refer to as *Five-level QDA* (Woolf, 2014; Woolf & Silver, in press), is not proposed as a new or different method of undertaking computer-assisted analysis, but rather as an exposition of the processes that expert CAQDAS users undertake unconsciously (see Figure 2).

The objective of *Five-level QDA* is to resolve the contrast between the emergent nature of the analytic strategies and the more cut-and-dried nature of the software tactics in a conscious and effective manner. The focus is on the process of translation between the units of analysis that comprise each individual analytic task, and the affordances of the software features (Gaver, 1991). For analytic tasks in which the units are *formally equivalent*, analogous to word-by-word translation from one language to another (Nida & Taber, 1969), the translation process is straightforward, and a software feature can be selected and used for the task in the obvious manner. For example, using Microsoft Word as an analogy, the cut and paste buttons can be

		FIVE-LEVEL QDA		
	two levels of strategy >>>>> *translated to* >>>>> *two levels of tactics*			
Level 1	Level 2	Level 3	Level 4	Level 5
Objectives:	Analytic plan:	Translation:	Selected tools:	Constructed tools:
The purpose and context of a project, usually expressed as a research question and methodology	The conceptual framework and resulting analytic tasks	Translating from analytic tasks to software tools, and translating the results back again	Individual software operations used in a straightforward way	Combinations of software operations, or software operations used in a custom way

Figure 2. *Five-level QDA.*

used in the obvious way to cut and then paste text to a different location in a document. This is referred to in *Five-level QDA* as using a *selected tool*. However, as a qualitative data analysis proceeds the units of analytic tasks may not be formally equivalent to any obvious software feature. Continuing the analogy with Microsoft Word, the formatting of the text to be cut may be different from the formatting of the location to which it will be pasted, and without knowledge of the several alternative ways to paste the formatting as well as the characters of text, the most straightforward use of the cut and paste buttons may lead to undesired formatting in the pasted location. Returning to CAQDAS packages, it is in analogous situations that many users move the analysis off the CAQDAS package and continue in Microsoft Word or Excel or use pen and paper, or alternatively use the CAQDAS package in ways that to some extent suppresses the more complex or emergent aspects of the analytic tasks. To use CAQDAS packages powerfully the translation process needs to become more sophisticated analogous to *dynamic equivalence* in language translation in which word-by-word translation is inadequate, and high quality translation requires finding 'just the right words' in the second language to produce the same effect in the reader as the words in the first language (Nida & Taber, 1969). In *Five-level QDA* this is referred to as using a *constructed tool*, which simply means using software features in combination or in unusual ways that may not be obvious from their presentation on the screen. Expert CAQDAS users have typically learned through long practice to unconsciously undertake either straightforward or sophisticated translation of analytic tasks into *selected* or *constructed tools* as necessary. The purpose of *Five-level QDA* is to accelerate the gaining of this expertise by making the translation process conscious and explicit, thereby prioritizing the agency of learners in harnessing software. In workshop contexts this means the role of the teacher as facilitator rather than instructor is emphasized.

Implementing Five-level QDA

We have developed the *Analytic Planning Worksheet* to explain and illustrate translation in the context of learners' own projects, and to enable learners to become proficient in the process. *Analytic Planning Worksheets* enable learners to differentiate between the two levels of strategy (*objectives* and *analytic plan*) and the two levels of tactics (*selected tools* and *constructed tools*), and to develop skills in *translating* analytic tasks into software operations.

Figure 3 illustrates part of an *Analytic Planning Worksheet*, showing one phase of action of a critical discourse analysis study. We document whole projects in this way, with one such worksheet for each phase of action, broken down into its constituent analytic tasks (Figure 3 illustrates three).

If a software feature exists that directly maps onto the analytic task, the translation process is straightforward and a tool can be selected to fulfil the task (as with the first analytic task in Figure 3). Where the analytic task is more complex and/or where there is no individual software feature available to fulfil it, a tool has to be constructed out of the use of more than one feature (as with the second and third analytic tasks in Figure 3). The purpose of the translation column in Figure 3 is to unpack this process. Where translation is straightforward, no additional work is required. However, where it is sophisticated because it is not immediately clear how to harness software features to fulfil an analytic task, an additional *Translation Worksheet* is used to explicate the analytic units, to evaluate software affordances, to

Project: "Theory-testing Critical Discourse Analysis" of Tony Blair's speeches post office, using MAXQDA v11
ANALYTIC PLANNING WORKSHEET: Phase 4

Level 1: OBJECTIVES	**RESEARCH QUESTIONS/OTHER OBJECTIVES:** To what extent are elements of Blair's rhetorical style, as identified by Fairclough in *New Labour, New Language*, 2000, identifiable in speeches he made during the 4 years after leaving office?	**METHODOLOGY/PRINCIPLES GUIDING QDA:** "Theory-testing Critical Discourse Analysis" of Fairclough's (2000) interpretation of Blair's rhetorical styles *as a distinctive repertoire*. Process informed by Rosalind Gill's Discourse Analysis process (in Bauer & Gaskell, 2000) but adapted to specifically test the applicability of Fairclough's (2000) theory of New Labour, New Language.
Level 2a: GENERAL ANALYTIC PLAN	**SUMMARY OF CONCEPTUAL FRAMEWORK** See Phase 3 Worksheet and graphic model developed in MAXQDA software project : (Phase 3) Conceptual Framework#1 CONCEPTS: 5 of 6 aspects of Fairclough's "Blair's Distinctive Repertoire" (Blair's Poetic, Conviction Politician, Getting Tough, Consensus Politician, the Normal Person) VARIABLES: Time since leaving office, Speech Topic/Genre, Speech Purpose. **PRIOR PHASES OF ACTION COMPLETED:** (Phase 1) Critical appraisal of Fairclough's interpretations, (Phase 1a:Action Arising) Refinement of research question, (Phase 2) Develop conceptual framework, (Phase 3) Construct dataset **CURRENT PHASE OF ACTION:** (Phase 4) Categorize speeches to relevant variables **NEXT PHASE OF ACTION ANTICIPATED:** First critical reading of speeches	

Level 2b: CURRENT SET OF ANALYTIC TASKS	**Level 3: TRANSLATION**	**Levels 4/5: SELECTED OR CONSTRUCTED SOFTWARE TOOLS (ST or CT)**
(First analytic task of current phase of action) **Incorporate speeches into MAXQDA project** (name speeches using consistent protocol that includes speech number, date of delivery and short descriptive title)	ST: no translation worksheet required	*Selected Tool:* Create DOCUMENT GROUPS for each year (to compare over time) and import speeches. (add number of speeches per year to DOCUMENT GROUP name)
(Second analytic task of current phase of action) **Assign relevant factual variables to speeches** (date, topic, genre, location, total running words, range of running words)	CT: see Translation Worksheet #4a	*Constructed Tool:* (two-step process) 1) Export DOCUMENT VARIABLES to Excel, remove system variables, add variables 2) Import DOCUMENT VARIABLES
(Third analytic task of current phase of action) **Create analytically meaningful sub-sets of data for later interrogation** (based on Speech Topics and Running Words Ranges)	CT: see Translation Worksheet #4b	*Constructed Tool:* (series of three-step processes) 1) Identify most frequent speech topics using STATISTIC OF DOCUMENT VARIABLES 2) ACTIVATE DOCUMENTS BY DOCUMENT VARIABLES 3) Create and rename DOCUMENT SETS - For most frequent Topic groups : Faith (N=7), Climate Change (N=8), Global Relations - comprising Europe OR Middle East OR Northern Ireland (N=6). Create control group of remaining speeches. - Repeat for each Running Word Range (in groups of 500 from >500 to 4000-4999)

ACTION ARISING / SUMMARY OF OR REFLECTIONS ABOUT THIS COMPLETED PHASE OF ACTION:
Speech Topic DOCUMENT SETS to constitute the main groups for comparison. Need to work out how to account for differences in length of speech when quantifying coding later. Next task of action, as planned: to critically read and summarize speeches, but will do this one Speech Topic at a time rather than in historic order of speech delivery.

Figure 3. *Five-level QDA* Analytic Planning Worksheet, example of one phase of action from a project using MAXQDA version 11.

select the software components to act upon, and finally to specify the sequence of software operations to undertake.[2]

Repeating the framing elements in each iteration of an *Analytic Planning Worksheet* (i.e. Level 1 and Level 2a) reflects the iterative nature of QDA, so that refinements following each phase of analysis is systematically documented. The *Analytic Planning Worksheet* for Phase 4 of the data analysis (see Figure 3) includes the refined research question. In practice, the *Analytic Planning Worksheets* for all phases would appear one after the other in a single continuous file to serve as a detailed audit-trail of the data analysis, allowing easy review of each iteration of the process.

Workshops modelled on the *Recurring Hourglass* design introduce the principles of *Five-level QDA* early during the introductory discussions about analytic contexts (Figure 1), and are revisited throughout. Learners begin filling out an *Analytic Planning Worksheet* after the first guided walk-through, once the architecture of the software has been illustrated in high-level overview. First they list Level 1 Objectives to identify what they plan to do in general terms in order to answer the research question. Later in the workshop they choose a phase of action to focus on, and transform the list-based analytic plan into a discrete set of tasks on their *Analytic Planning Worksheet*. This serves to focus attention on designing analytic tasks to be effected in software with regard to the strategies (the project objectives), rather than the tactics (the features of the software).

In two-day workshops participants revisit their *Analytic Planning Worksheet* several times, making alterations as required, and as the workshop progresses they begin filling out the software operations column in light of what they are learning about the program capabilities. The focus of day-two is hands-on work to put their plans into practice.

The adaptability of Five-level QDA

This paper has focused on illustrating the implementation of *Five-level QDA* within two-day intensive CAQDAS workshops. However, *Five-level QDA* can be adapted to different learning contexts. It has been successfully implemented in face-to-face workshops with groups varying from 5 to 14 participants, and over one or two days, and in remote coaching sessions delivered via Skype with both teams and individual researchers. It is also being written in textbook format for researchers already familiar with the basic operations of their chosen software who wish to accelerate the transition from basic to advanced use of the program (Woolf & Silver, in press). As well as using the textbook to augment our own teaching, *Five-level QDA* can be adopted by other CAQDAS teachers and learners.

Conclusion

Our combined trajectories of almost 40 years of CAQDAS teaching highlight the pedagogical challenges of developing learners' expertise in the powerful use of these software packages. The fast pace of software development as well as the rise of mixed methods, secondary analysis, and longitudinal qualitative research, have increased researchers' expectations of CAQDAS (Paulus et al., 2014; Silver & Lewins, 2014). Additionally, a new generation of digital-native students expect computer-assisted solutions in all fields, including qualitative data analysis. Yet CAQDAS teaching is not widely embedded in higher education, as demonstrated by the high proportion of postgraduate students attending workshops: 68% of CNP workshop attendees in the 2013–2014 academic year (Silver & Rivers, 2014).

Increased demand for CAQDAS teaching has been accompanied by two trends that created distinct pedagogical challenges: increasing complexity of CAQDAS packages and increasing diversity amongst users and uses to which software is put. Complexity brings benefits of broader applicability, extension of analytic possibilities, mixing of techniques and collaborative working. The challenge for learners is in uncovering appropriate pathways to undertaking systematic and rigorous analysis. Because there are now so many alternative ways to execute particular analytic tasks, confusion is common (Silver & Rivers, 2014). The pedagogical challenge is to enable learners to traverse software complexities and employ their features appropriately.

The growing diversity of user needs and uses of CAQDAS has resulted in an increasingly heterogeneous population of learners seeking instruction in open-registration workshops, the mainstay of CAQDAS teaching. Certainly there are pedagogical advantages to this heterogeneity: diversity in project characteristics exposes learners' to a range of research contexts and illustrates the importance of harnessing CAQDAS features specifically to the requirements of each analytic task, and novice researchers benefit from hearing about the practices and experiences of more experienced researchers. However, diversity increases the challenge of ensuring each learners' needs are met.

It is common to address diversity by developing a 'one-size-fits-all' method for using CAQDAS that presents a generic set of computer-assisted QDA procedures applicable to all learners, methodologies and projects.[3] However, our experience convinces us that this is neither feasible nor appropriate (Lewins & Silver, 2007) and to varying extents suppresses the iterative and emergent nature of QDA (Woolf, 2014). A 'one-size-fits-all' approach implies that the use of software itself constitutes a method of analysis, but just as there is no one method of QDA, there is no one method of using software. Our trajectory of pedagogic development has moved in the opposite direction, by increasingly *facilitating* learners to harness software appropriately for their specific requirements, rather than *instructing* them in a method of use. However, this is no easy matter given the complex task of applying cut-and-dried computer software to the emergent activity of QDA. We are encouraged that *Five-level QDA* is proving successful in our own practices, by continuing the transition from instruction to facilitation through emphasizing learner agency in harnessing CAQDAS packages appropriately for the chosen methodology and type of research project.

We hope that our experiences will support teachers in meeting the increasingly demanding needs of CAQDAS learners. *Five-level QDA* is our response to the need for an effective CAQDAS pedagogy, and is being developed as a full curriculum that can be adopted across methodologies, software packages and teaching modes (Woolf & Silver, in press). We will continue to critically reflect on this pedagogy and test its implementation in a variety of contexts in the years to come.

Disclosure statement

No potential conflict of interest was reported by the authors.

Notes

1. Established in 1994 the CAQDAS Networking Project provides independent information, advice, training and on-going support in the range of CAQDAS packages. http://www.surrey.ac.uk/sociology/research/researchcentres/caqdas/.
2. It is outside the scope of this article to illustrate *Translation Worksheets* but these are illustrated in full in Woolf and Silver (in press).
3. We refer to this as *Three-level QDA*, but it is beyond the scope of this article to go further into this approach to teaching CAQDAS (see Woolf, 2014; Woolf & Silver, in press).

References

Ausubel, D. P., & Robinson, F. G. (1969). *School learning – An introduction to educational psychology*. New York, NY: Holt, Rinehart & Winston.

Bransford, J. D., Sherwood, R. D., Hasselbring, T. S., Kinzer, C. K., & Williams, S. M. (1990). Anchored instruction: Why we need it and how technology can help. In D. Nix & R. Spiro (Eds.), *Cognition, education, and multimedia: Exploring ideas in high technology* (pp. 115–141). Hillsdale, NJ: Lawrence Erlbaum Associates.

Davis, H., & Krayer, A. (2014, July). *Embedding NVivo in postgraduate research training*. Paper presented at the 6th National Centre for Research Methods (NCRM) Research Methods Festival. University of Oxford, Oxford.

di Gregorio, S. (2014, May). *Time for a new pedagogic approach to teaching CAQDAS*. Paper presented at CAQDAS 2014 Conference: Past, Present and Future: 25 years of CAQDAS. University of Surrey, Guildford.

di Gregorio, S., & Davidson, J. (2008). *Qualitative research design for software users*. Maidenhead: Open University Press.

Fielding, N., & Lee, R. M. (1991). *Using computers in qualitative research*. Newbury Park, CA: Sage.

Friese, S. (2014). *Qualitative data analysis with ATLAS.ti*. London: Sage.

Gaver, W. W. (1991, March). Technology affordances. In *Proceedings of the SIGCHI Conference on Human Factors In Computing Systems* (pp. 79–84). New York, NY: ACM.

Gibbs, G. (2014). *Count: Developing STEM skills in qualitative research methods teaching and learning*. York: Higher Education Academy. Retrieved from http://eprints.hud.ac.uk/22751/

Honey, P., & Mumford, A. (1982). *Manual of learning styles*. London: P Honey.

Kaczynski, D., & Kelly, M. (2004, November). *Curriculum development for teaching qualitative data analysis online*. Paper presented at QualIT2004: International Conference on Qualitative Research in IT & IT in Qualitative Research. Brisbane, Australia.

Kilburn, D., Nind, M., & Wiles, R. (2014). Learning as researchers and teachers: The development of a pedagogical culture for social science research methods? *British Journal of Educational Studies, 62*, 191–207.

Kolb, D. (1984). *Experiential learning: Experience as the source of learning and development*. Englewood Cliffs, NJ: Prentice-Hall.

Lave, J., & Wenger, E. (1991). *Situated learning*. Cambridge: Cambridge University Press.

Lewins, A., & Silver, C. (2007). *Using software in qualitative research*. London: Sage.

Luttwak, E. N. (2001). *Strategy: The logic of peace and war* (2nd ed.). Cambridge, MA: Harvard University Press.

Mayer, R. E. (1979). Can advance organizers influence meaningful learning? *Review of Educational Research, 49*, 371–383.

Nida, E. A., & Taber, C. R. (1969). *The theory and practice of translation*. Leiden: E. J. Brill.

Paulus, T. M., Lester, J. N., & Dempster, P. G. (2014). *Digital tools for qualitative research*. Thousand Oaks, CA: Sage.

Reigeluth, C. M. (1979). In search of a better way to organize instruction: The elaboration theory. *Journal of Instructional Development, 2*, 8–15.

Silver, C. (2010). *Research design for longitudinal case-study project: Tracking the use of software in real projects using different methodologies*. Guildford: QUIC Briefing Paper, Qualitative Innovations in CAQDAS (QUIC), The CAQDAS Networking Project, University of Surrey, UK.

Silver, C., & Lewins, A. (2014). *Using software in qualitative research: A step-by-step guide* (2nd ed.). London: Sage.

Silver, C., & Rivers, C. (2014). *Learning from the learners: The role of technology acceptance and adoption theories in understanding researchers' early experiences with CAQDAS packages*. ATLAS.ti User Conference 2013: Fostering Dialog on Qualitative Methods, Technische Universität Berlin. Berlin: Universitätsverlag der TU Berlin. Retrieved from http://nbn-resolving.de/urn:nbn:de:kobv:83-opus4-44300

Silver, C., & Rivers, C. B. (2014). The CAQDAS postgraduate learning model: An interplay between methodological awareness, analytic adeptness and technological proficiency. *International Journal of Social Research Methodology*.

Smith, P. L., & Ragan, T. J. (2005). *Instructional design*. Hoboken, NJ: Wiley.

Whitehead, A. N. (1929). *The aims of education and other essays*. New York, NY: The Free Press.

Woolf, N. (2014). *Analytic strategies and analytic tactics*. Paper presented at the ATLAS.ti User Conference 2013: Fostering Dialog on Qualitative Methods, Technische Universität Berlin. Berlin: Universitätsverlag der TU Berlin. Retrieved from http://nbn-resolving.de/urn:nbn:de:kobv:83-opus4-44159

Woolf, N. H., & Silver, C. (in press). *Five-level QDA: A method for learning to use QDA software powerfully*. Santa Barbara, CA: Woolf Publishing.

Learning to manage and share data: jump-starting the research methods curriculum

Louise Corti and Veerle Van den Eynden

UK Data Archive, University of Essex, Colchester, Essex, UK

> Researchers' responsibilities towards their research data are changing across all domains of social scientific endeavour. Government, funders and publishers expect greater transparency of, open access to, and re-use of research data, and fears over data loss call for more robust information security practices. Researchers must develop, enhance and professionalise their research data management skills to meet these challenges and to deal with a changing data sharing environment. This paper sets out how we have contributed to jump-starting the research methods training curriculum in this field by translating high-level needs into practical guidance and training activities. Our pedagogical approach involves applicable, easy-to-digest, modules based on best practice guidance for managing and sharing research data. In line with recent findings on successful practices in methods teaching, we work on the principle of embedding grounded learning activities within existing narratives of research design and implementation.

Introduction

Across the disciplinary spectrum, researchers' responsibilities towards their own research data and their use of others' data are changing. Open access is increasingly mandated for publicly-funded research data, governments demand transparency in research they support, and publishers ask for evidence of data that underpin findings. The economic climate also requires more re-use of data. In turn, concerns about data loss call for more robust information security practices. Much of the responsibility for the management of research data is placed upon researchers who need to improve, enhance and professionalise their skills to meet the challenge of producing the highest quality research data for publication, sharing and reuse in a responsible way. Since data form the cornerstone of empirical research, such data skills must be integrated with research methods teaching and learning. Novice researchers at undergraduate or postgraduate level may benefit from teaching that is integrated into degree curricula and sits naturally alongside narratives of standard methodological approaches. Experienced researchers are likely to need a greater degree of upskilling, to plug gaps in current knowledge and refresh or update their knowledge in response to rapid changes in technology or legislation relating to the governance of

---

This is an Open Access article distributed under the terms of the Creative Commons Attribution License (http://creativecommons.org/licenses/by/4.0/), which permits unrestricted use, distribution, and reproduction in any medium, provided the original work is properly cited.

research data. Irrespective of the level of a researcher's expertise, these skills can help maximise the impact of research and foster greater appreciation of the use of secondary sources. However, guidance and training for gaining data management and sharing skills are noticeably absent from many social science research methods curricula, with the exception of data handling covered within statistical analytical techniques. Data management skills are equally important for qualitative researchers. A culture change is therefore needed and pedagogy forms part of that change.

In this paper we show how research methods training can be enhanced by integrating practical guidance and training activities into research methods instructional literature and teaching. In this approach, upskilling can be achieved by interweaving modular practice-based instruction in data management with traditional methods learning that focuses on research design, fieldwork and analysis. As we move into a growing data landscape with novel forms of data coming on stream, these skills represent a step change towards the next level of competence required for data mining and data science.

Our pedagogical approach involves up-to-date, easy-to-digest information about practices for managing and sharing a variety of types of research data, presented in a modular structure. In line with recent findings on successful practices in methods teaching, we work on the principle of embedding grounded learning activities within the narrative of research design and implementation (Buckley, Brown, Thomson, Olsen, & Carter, 2015). Effective learning of data skills within social science research methods teaching was found by Kilburn, Nind, and Wiles (2014a) to be achieved through three means: active learning by making processes visible; directly experiencing methods; and critical reflection on practice. Providing building blocks that create a solid empirically-based research knowledge base to underpin the creation and use of digital data in the social sciences is at the heart of our approach. A modular structure is also beneficial because it enables the coverage of topics to be tailored towards multi- or non-disciplinary learners. Case studies, practical activities, exercises and group discussions help support effective learning and application of the core concepts. Success of the approach has been demonstrated through a grant from the UK Economic and Social Research Council's (ESRC) Research Development Initiative to refine and test the teaching materials and by integration of content and pedagogy into more recent publication of an internationally-appealing handbook on the topic (Corti, Van den Eynden, Bishop, & Woollard, 2014).

Challenges for data management pedagogy

Emerging agendas for data sharing

In the past 5 years, significant funds have been made available to open up a variety of data for research purposes, such as government administrative data, data underlying published research outputs and data from commercial sources. The rise of the 'big data' agenda has also pushed to the fore the issue of how to look after and manage data to benefit interdisciplinary investigation of large and complex data. In the UK, funding is being dedicated to secondary analysis research, with the intention of maximising opportunities for the analysis of data from large-scale government investments such as national surveys and cohort studies (ESRC, 2012). With a decrease in funding for research generating new data, it is important for researchers to explore the optimal use of existing data. Investments that seek to advance data-related skills are also being driven by research councils' policies on open access

(Research Councils UK [RCUK], 2012) and by the desire to enhance quantitative skills in social science education (British Academy, 2014). These sets of activities would appear to benefit greatly from alignment around shareable data as a focus for training in the collection, management, and analysis of long-term data resources.

Skills involved in data management

While data management skills come under the broad banner of data handling, they fit in at all stages of the research process. Figure 1 shows likely intervention points in the data lifecycle of data management type activities that should be considered in any research design and throughout the research process.

Based on the UK Data Archive's decennia of work supporting and advising ESRC grant holders about data archiving, sharing, and reuse, within the framework of the ESRC research data policy, this framework was translated into guidance that followed the logic of the data lifecycle. Guidance was iterated, enhanced and expanded into detailed best practice guidance for researchers and accompanying teaching materials and further development resulted in an extensive handbook on best practices for managing and sharing research data (Corti et al., 2014). The content includes:

- the importance of sharing data;
- consent, confidentiality and ethics of data sharing;
- rights associated with the use of existing data;
- describing, contextualising, and documenting research data;
- data formats and software;
- storage, back-up and security in response to the fragility of digital data;
- publishing data in a sustainable way and enabling future citation.

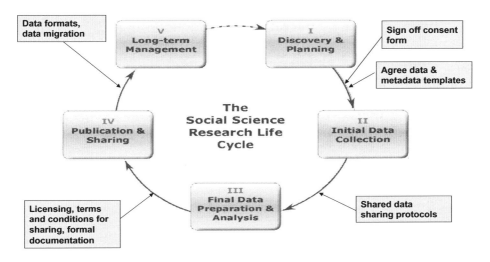

Figure 1. Intervention points in the research data lifecycle. Based on Green and Gutman (2006).

Proficiency in these topics is expected for those creating new data during the course of research and those undertaking secondary analysis. Enhanced data skills become essential as we move towards a new data landscape where more digital data are increasingly available for use, including new forms of data such as social media discussions, administrative data, commercial customer data and epidemiological data. Such novel data sources are already entering the social sciences via new data centres dedicated to the challenges of solving research challenges using 'big data' (ESRC, 2013). In the future we are likely to see increased analysis of large and varied data sources in the pursuit of impactful findings.

Data handling in methods teaching: assessing gaps

Data handling methods have tended to be more widely acknowledged in disciplines where large-scale secondary data sources are routinely used. Our own experience tells us that, for example, geographers and historians tend to have good data skills and are familiar with reusing and sharing research data. Secondary analysis of survey data is routinely taught, and here data management skills such as quality assurance measures, metadata and annotation of data, formatting and modes of organisation are very much part of research and learning activities. Assessment of data created by someone else is a useful way to gain insight into what it means to prepare data for sharing and future use. In turn, economists may have good technical data skills, but sometimes lack appreciation of ethical issues surrounding data obtained from human participants (Blomfield, 2012). Other research domains may suffer from a tendency to exclude technical components from methods courses. For instance, students of sociology or linguistics may only encounter data handling in the context of collecting data for their own research projects.

Despite reviews of postgraduate training guidelines and surveys of senior academics and researchers over the past 10 years, the UK still fails to produce enough quantitatively proficient or data-savvy graduates in some areas of social sciences (MacInnes, 2012). From an international perspective, the quantitative skills deficit was also recognised as a major concern in the 2010 *International Benchmarking Review of Sociology* (ESRC, BSA, & HAPS, 2010). This recognition by research funders and professional societies propagated a welcomed flurry of activity (British Academy, 2012; Nuffield Foundation, 2012; Royal Statistical Society, 2014; Williams, Payne, Hodgkinson, & Poole, 2008). Concrete investments have followed, with some £20million invested in the UK's recent Q-Step initiative that aims to achieve a life-course approach to building quantitative methods skills (Nuffield Foundation, 2013). The UK's ESRC National Centre for Research Methods (NCRM) is also supported to initiate and promote targeted and advanced methods training across the methods spectrum (NCRM, 2014). This drive to embed methods in real social science questions and engage in practice-based learning rings well with our own approach. However, it would be beneficial for these programmes to explicitly consider the longer-term value and re-use of data.

Of most interest to the thrust of this paper were the findings emerging from the 2012 Higher Education Academy Social Sciences learning and teaching summit, focusing on teaching research methods in the social sciences. These included innovative ways of improving applied research methods, for example by gaining experience outside of the academic environment and undertaking projects in the work place (Hamilton, Gossman, & Southern, 2014; Kirton, Campbell, & Hardwick,

2014). These offer working models of applied methods in practice. Others have identified real life problems and task-oriented group work as a means of engaging reluctant students with research methods teaching (Leston-Bandera, 2013).

We have seen some progress in the uptake of secondary analysis, particularly for qualitative researchers. The outreach work done by the UK Data Service and its predecessors in providing teaching resources and running training courses encourage uptake of secondary analyses for qualitative data (Bishop, 2012). This included collating case studies from academics who use secondary data in their own teaching (UK Data Service, 2014c). A recent review of research methods learning and teaching also recognised the opportunities of using existing data as a learning tool in methods teaching – either working with own data that learners bring to a session, or using teachers' data or teaching datasets, the latter being easier to manage (Kilburn, Nind, & Wiles, 2014b). Across the curricula, though, there remains work to be done on streamlining the portfolio of data management skills within research methods teaching.

The supporting research methods literature

The recent research methods literature continues to comprise publications that predominantly focus on research design, data collection in the field and data analysis, although the availability of instructional books on secondary analysis techniques is growing (Smith, 2008; Trzesniewski, Donnellamn, & Lucas, 2011; Vartanian, 2010). However, the social science literature still lacks texts that cover the core skills required to support good data management and sharing. Some of these skills are inherently taken for granted as good research practice. Yet issues such as file format choices, storage, backup and security of research data, and documentary descriptions of data, are crucial in creating high quality data. So too are ethical and legal considerations in data use and stewardship – both within and beyond the life of project. In particular, qualitative researchers may find few written sources on managing digital data for sharing. Authors of new instructional methods books should be encouraged to include such topics.

Upskilling for novel forms of data

In the 'big data' era, researchers see the benefits of working with novel and more complex data sources, often across disciplinary boundaries. With this, there is potential for deficits in confidence or skills for researchers to become even greater. While some disciplines may feel comfortable running algorithms on big data, many social scientists will want to take smaller samples and analyse these in more familiar ways. Examples are seen in the use of social media data such as Twitter feeds, where a discourse analyst may wish to select tweets from a particular social group, geographical context, or pertaining to a specific issue.

Good metadata and quality assurance skills are needed for retrieving, assessing, manipulating, and analysing these big data extracts; skills that fall under the rubric of data management. Courses aimed at non-technical audiences are emerging on the use of social media data, such as network analysis and data mining. These courses will also introduce skills on data extraction using Application Programming Interfaces and assessing the quality of new forms of data by means of statistical techniques (University of Michigan, 2014; University of Southampton, 2014).

For instance, research on smart cities demands much greater appreciation of data modelling, which is best achieved through cross-disciplinary methodological collaboration (Urban Big Data Centre, 2014).

For the qualitative researcher wishing to explore the potential of online digital textual sources – be those social media data or other source – the upskilling needed to handle, extract and analyse such data may be significant. Basic core data management skills can bring researchers some steps closer to technical proficiency. For instance, a successful outcome might be for a biographical researcher to run algorithms on large volumes of rich text relevant to their area of study.

Despite the trends towards exploiting 'big data', users of 'smaller' data should not be left by the wayside. While small scale research will remain critical, researchers who perhaps consider that big data pushes them out of their comfort zone can benefit from upskilling. Enabling them to feel comfortable with handling complex and new forms of research data, to be cognisant of longer-term sustainability of data, and to appreciate the art of accessing and re-use of secondary data sources are all significant steps towards this goal. This incremental knowledge sharing and capacity building will help the broader social science research community move towards appreciating big data.

Looking to the more data-intensive disciplines, the new data science courses aimed at computer or statistics students all take for granted some areas of data management skills with their modules mostly oriented towards data handling, quality assessment and analytics. However, it may be some time before undergraduate courses in traditional social science disciplines embrace such technical components. Even in our own institution, where data science courses have recently started up, the social sciences do not yet contribute to that teaching with students instead hailing from maths and computing programmes. The emergence of internet-based text as a data source is prompting qualitative social scientists to consider branching into new types of analysis, requiring more advanced computational skills which may benefit from structured training in the context of degree courses.

In summary, the UK's apparent quantitative methods skills deficit, together with demands of the current research climate (openness, accountability, impact and value for money) and the need for computational skills in the era of big data, emphasise the importance of data management skills. To meet this need, methods curricula must evolve rapidly.

Applying solutions: data management skills, training, teaching and learning
Professional training in data management for researchers

Sharing data is becoming a vital part of research activity. This is especially true if we consider the training needs of professional researchers and their requirement for life-long learning to keep pace with the changing demands of social research and the UK research councils' expectations for societal and economic impact (Research Councils UK, 2011).

Over the past 5 years we have seen a rise in the marketing of career development pathways and support for junior researchers. Vitae (2013), an international programme led by a UK charity and supported by UK research and higher educational funding, is dedicated to realising the potential of researchers through transforming their professional and career development. In their role of supporting the employability of doctoral researchers, Vitae concentrates on enhancing research skills.

However, a review of their 2008–2012 framework and concordat indicates that, while employability of postgraduates is high on their agenda, there is no mention of the need for data competence or management skills across the disciplines.

Social science libraries also play a role in offering support to students in gathering references for assignments and in some cases actively helping with statistical projects. In the US there has long existed the specific role of the data librarian, working to deliver access to data and even teaching appropriate techniques for statistical analysis. Evidence from Corti and Watkins (2004) suggested that in the US, where there is typically a heavier focus on quantitative methods training in social science courses, students needing guidance with statistical assignments turned to their local data librarians for assistance. Consequently, a movement of dedicated extra-curricular training by data librarians to support these skills has developed.

In the UK, the Jisc (the lead organisation that champions the use of digital technologies in UK education and research) invested in a 5 year Managing Research Data programme (2009–2013) to help develop and deliver data infrastructure, resources, tools and training materials to meet the increasing demands of research funders for good data management or sharing of research data in the higher education sector. This resulted in various UK institutions developing and investing in institutional research data policies, data repositories and data management training resources. Examples include the Universities of Edinburgh and Bristol, where materials were developed partially based on the UK Data Service training modules (UK Data Service, 2014b; University of Bristol, 2014; University of Edinburgh, 2014). The Digital Curation Centre provides an overview of data management training provided for researchers and data custodians, such as library and research support staff across UK institutions (DCC, 2013). The UK Data Service runs a national programme of training for researchers and research support staff (UK Data Service, 2014b, 2014c).

There are also an increasing number of training courses on the topic of digital preservation (now a discipline in its own right). Training in digital preservation is aimed at information and IT professionals, as well as archivists and curators of digital heritage and collections, rather than researchers exclusively. These seek to provide hands-on knowledge and skills involving the collection, selection, management, long-term preservation and accessibility of digital assets. Examples are the Digital Preservation Coalition training courses in the UK (Digital Preservation Coalition [DPC], 2014) and the Library of Congress's Digital Preservation Outreach and Education Programme in the US (Library of Congress, 2013). Some master programmes for archivists now cover useful aspects of data management, though are unlikely to be grounded in a narrative of social science research.

In summary, courses on data management for sharing are emerging in academic institutions in the UK and US, motivated by research funders' data policies. Europe is lagging behind, largely due to the absence of funder data policies and the drivers these bring.

A modular strategy for introducing data management skills

Doctoral training in methods has drastically changed in the last few years, with a move away from ad hoc supervisor–student training towards institutionally organised training, making use of short and professional development courses, hands-on sessions and small group work, plus case studies critique (Kilburn et al., 2014b; Kottmann, 2011; Sloan, 2013; Strayhorn, 2009).

Examples of teaching advanced quantitative methods using a modular approach can be found in the online courses for multi-level modelling provided by the Learning Environment for Multilevel Modelling (LEMMA) (Centre for Multilevel Modelling, 2014). LEMMA offers a set of graduated modules starting from an introduction to quantitative research progressing to multilevel modelling of continuous and binary data. Equally, In the US the Interuniversity Consortium for Political and Social Research's Data-Driven Learning Guides enhance teaching of core concepts making use of topics drawn from concepts that are included in introductory-level social science textbooks (Inter-University Consortium for Political and Social Research, 2009). Their guides are topic-based and pose research questions that could be explored using a particular data-set, An example is the Guide on *Age and Attitudes about the Rights of Homosexuals* which investigates trends in attitudes regarding the rights of homosexuals in the United States from the early 1990s to 2007, using the longitudinal Houston Area Survey. The module guides users to work through the questions, prompting them to recode the data, available via an online browser, to be able to answer substantive questions of interest. Commentary is provided taking the reader through analytical issues relevant to the data, such as inference and weighting, and provides a summary of key findings.

In developing research data management training materials on a range of modular topics, that can complement methods teaching in quantitative and qualitative research methods, we have formulated a flexible toolkit that can be incorporated into undergraduate, masters, and doctoral taught curricula. These modules can also be used as voluntary symposia, doctoral colloquia, or professional development sessions. While the skills require some degree of research methods knowledge, they remain accessible to second or third year undergraduate students.

Over the years, our training workshops on managing and sharing research data have developed to achieve effective learning of data skills, following the forms that are recognised in existing literature on research methods teaching: active learning by making processes visible; directly experiencing methods; and critical reflection on practice (Kilburn et al., 2014a). Active learning is realised through the use of numerous practical tasks, exercises and discussions during training sessions, such as hands-on lab exercises in encryption of sensitive data files, creation of metadata using existing software tools, anonymisation of interview transcripts and survey tables, and quizzes on data practices in collaborative research. Learning by doing or experiencing is applied where trainees develop their own data management plans throughout training sessions. Critical reflection on data practices is supported through group discussions of real-case data challenges, such as the ethical implications of sharing confidential data or copyright scenarios, or discussions around individual's own data requirements to explore shared challenges.

Our modules consist of theoretical presentations, hands-on exercises or scenarios and quizzes (with answers) to practice understanding of topics we consider essential in conducting research, efficient collaborative working, and undertaking informed secondary analysis. The modularised topics are: why and how to share research data; planning data management; documenting and contextualising data; formatting data; storing, backing-up and transferring data; ethics, consent and confidentiality; and copyright of data (Corti et al., 2014).

These modules were road-tested and fine-tuned into flexible training materials through use in over 75 hands-on workshops to audiences of doctoral students, researchers and research support staff over the period 2008–2013. Research methods trainers can adapt and repurpose presentations and exercises to suit their own discipline, country, or relevant laws. The resources are downloadable via our website. Although the resources were primarily developed for social scientists, they are broad enough to be used by other disciplines including the natural sciences, arts and humanities.

Fitting modules to the audience

In running training sessions, we adapt programmes to suit our audience. For example, for a two-hour doctoral professionalisation workshop for social scientists, time would permit a presentation and an exercise on gaining consent for collecting, using and sharing qualitative data from structuring interviews in the form of well-documented and well-formatted transcripts. A half-day workshop might focus on several technical modules on formatting and organising, storing, and documenting data, as a continuous professional development course. The use of suggestive titles like *Are you looking after your research data properly?* help to attract audiences.

Some topics lend themselves better to facilitated group discussions, such as sharing experiences of managing data-rich projects. More technical areas, such as data storage or encryption, may benefit from relatable anecdotes of data disasters in presentations and the realisation of understanding through light-hearted quizzes, so as to keep learners engaged.

Here we provide four examples of how a specific audience can be taught the core skills within a set time frame. We discuss the most successful trajectory for delivery of these modules, when to condense or lengthen them, and what kind of activities work best in particular settings. The following workshop examples a two hour overview session to an intensive two-day workshop.

(1) Two-hour taster session for students (second year undergraduates onwards) on *Looking after your research data*:

- Introduction to data managing and sharing, planning data management: *presentation*.
- Data storage, back-up, security, transmission, encryption, file sharing: *presentation, exercise, quiz and tools demonstration*.
- Quality control, version control, formatting, describing and organising data: *presentation, Q&A and quiz*.

(2) Half-day training for social science professionals/ethics committee members on: *Managing and sharing research data: legal and ethical issues*:

- Data management and data sharing applied to research involving people as participants: legal and ethical aspects of data sharing (based on UK legislation and requirements for publically funded research) and data management planning: *presentation and Q&A*.
- Developing consent agreements for obtaining informed consent from participants to share data: *presentation, exercise, group discussion*.
- Dealing with confidential research information and anonymisation techniques to enable use and sharing of research data: *presentation, exercise, group discussion*.

(3) One-day training for social science and humanities research students on *Going digital: Looking after and managing your digital research data*:

- Benefits of data management and data management planning: *presentation and discussion.*
- Documenting your data: *presentation.*
- Creating metadata for a data collection: *practical lab session with exercises.*
- Storing data, data security, formatting, encrypting, organising data: *presentation, software demonstrations and Q&A.*
- Encrypting files, backups, checksums: *practical lab session with exercises.*
- Copyright and IPR: *presentation and scenarios for group discussion.*
- Ethical and legal aspects – key messages for sharing data: *presentation and scenarios for group discussion.*
- Data management planning: *presentation and write a data management plan exercise.*

(4) Two-day train the trainers event on *Looking after and managing your research data.*

- Overview of the UK Data Archive's managing and sharing training materials: *presentation.*
- Practical data management planning and funder policy context: *presentation and exercises.*
- Consent and ethics: *presentation and group exercises.*
- Data anonymisation: *presentation and group exercises.*
- Formatting data: *presentation, formats quiz, file naming and transcription exercises.*
- Documenting and contextualising your data: *presentation and context exercise.*
- Data copyright: *presentation and research scenario discussions.*
- Storing and transferring data and data security: *presentation, software demonstrations and quiz.*
- Training clinics: *discuss your personal data needs with the trainers.*

In these sessions, we observe that group work is important and can greatly aid the learning experience.

To incorporate such data management training into taught courses that may be constrained in terms of time or curriculum space, the modules fit alongside new and existing training provision. At undergraduate level, the typical 10-week course on quantitative methods likely does not have enough time to include data skills that sit outside the confines of data collection and analysis. For qualitative methods courses, a ten-week course has barely enough time to cover the practicalities of collecting, transcribing, analysing and reporting research data. At masters and doctoral level, it may become feasible to include half-day or one-day data skills training. As we suggested above, flexibility may be the key, for example adding appealing workshop activities to mainstream courses.

One of the most positive outcomes of teaching these materials has been the positive reception of qualitative researchers to distinct topics that might otherwise be deemed out of their comfort zone. At the same time, using real life examples of research that are relevant and topical can aid qualitative researchers to fully engage with some of the more technical topics. For areas like ethics and consent or interview transcription, qualitative researchers may feel more confident engaging, perhaps even by reflecting on and challenging their own everyday practices (like only seeking consent for sole access to data, thereby precluding colleagues and research students from using their data in the future). However, topics like data security, encryption in transferring disclosive data between colleagues, and creating metadata can appear technically difficult. By engaging participants in practical and relevant activities we can demystify the complexity of some of the more technical digital data practices or perceived heavyweight topics, supporting learners in gaining these essential practical skills.

Who is best placed to teach?

Questions may be raised over whether methods teachers or research support staff are best placed to teach these materials, or whether learners should attend face-to-face training or self-study. Encouragingly, we have seen interesting examples of academics teaching research methods being creative in their classes by incorporating data reuse assignments that enable critical evaluation of secondary data and exposure to other researchers' data (Haynes & Jones, 2012; Kelly, 2012; Smith, 2008; Turton, 2012). Moreover, emerging literature on re-use of qualitative data, such as in a 2012 Special Issue of this journal on working with archived textual and visual material in social research helps to inspire students about the possibilities of confronting data they have not collected themselves (Crow & Edwards, 2012; Kynaston, 2005; Corti, Witzel, & Bishop, 2005).

Alternatively it may be that it is not the responsibility of methods teachers to cover these skills, but that of professional skills trainers. Many universities have set up skills-oriented courses to help amplify their students' employment prospects and to support lifelong learning. For example, SCONUL (2014), as an academic library-based enterprise, aims to support both research excellence and students' academic success and employability. They cover important areas of information and digital literacy. In the past year the topic of data management has been added to their list of priority areas. Indeed there is no reason why data management skills could not be run as a parallel track to any kind of employability or professional development-oriented training.

Finally, there is also the role of institutional or faculty research offices that are already charged with offering support to researchers on funding opportunities, grant applications and research ethics submissions; as well as providing training on academic skills such as writing grant applications and academic writing. As their portfolio of support has increased to provide active advice for writing data management plans, training on some data skills could be handled by them. Skills could include writing data management planning, costing for data management in grant applications, and ethical issues in collecting and reusing data. In similar ways, information systems service providers in universities can provide expertise and training in the more technical aspects of data management and sharing, such as good practices in data storage, backup, data encryption, data security measures and data transferring.

One of the greatest challenges of teaching on these topics is ensuring the link with current research practice (and therefore trainers' familiarity with research practices). Success may depend on the experience of the trainers and on their ability to speak the language of research of their audience; being confident to answer questions about ethics, fieldwork procedures, data validation and so on. Ultimately, any of these actors are capable of teaching data management skills to students and researchers. The availability of teaching materials and exercises such as those presented by the authors enables many professionals to take on this form of teaching, either as part of or complementing the research methods curriculum.

Conclusion

Researchers are expected to adapt to new ways of working with data that require skills to accompany their existing analytics techniques. Data management skills can be seen as the building blocks for data science and in turn, a core set of skills for social scientists rather than the domain of dedicated data managers. All empirical researchers are data managers to some degree. As data sharing requirements come into play, many placing the research institution at the heart of responsibility for data sharing (EPSRC, 2011), the pressure to build capacity amongst staff and researchers across all research disciplines in data management is increasingly crucial. Trained teaching, research, and support staff can engage students and learners in data management, beginning a cycle of upskilling. Training provision for managing and sharing data is emerging at a fairly rapid pace, led by institutions charged with overseeing the sharing of data by researchers, in turn driven by conditions of funding for their research projects. However, a cultural change is still needed to encourage research methods teachers and trainers to embrace and capitalise on this emerging field of pedagogy.

In this paper we set out to demonstrate teaching strategies that can help enhance social scientists' data management skills. Higher-level needs of gaining proficiency and confidence in digital data handling can be met by translating them into practical guidance and training activities that embed into research (see also Silver & Woolf, 2015). With the uptake of these strategies in the UK and beyond, this approach is contributing to jump-starting the research methods curriculum for data management. At its heart, this pedagogy relies on easy-to-digest information on considered topics, coupled with grounded activities that reflect either the substantive or methodological interests of learners. Where possible, such modular activities complement existing research methods training approaches and instructional literature. Be it the ethical aspects of data sharing, collecting and entering data using software packages, or the importance of data documentation, all parts of research design and analysis have short and longer-term data management implications.

Finally, with pressure for more transparency in research, for increased reuse of existing data, and for handling confidential data well, the pedagogical approach outlined in this paper offer skills that can help researchers move more readily and confidently into this space. These transferable skills help researchers to be better organised in dealing with digital data sources, and be better prepared to work within ethical and legal frameworks that govern research data. Further, they offer a strategic contribution to the UK's research capacity building programme in the social sciences.

Acknowledgements

We would like to acknowledge our colleagues who have undertaken training in areas of research data management at the UK Data Archive, in particular, Libby Bishop who contributed to our training modules and the 2014 handbook on Managing and Sharing Data.

Disclosure statement

No potential conflict of interest was reported by the authors.

References

Bishop, L. (2012). Using archived qualitative data for teaching: Practical and ethical considerations. *International Journal of Social Research Methodology, 15*, 341–350. doi:10.1080/13645579.2012.688335

Blomfield, M. (2012). Ethics in economics: Lessons from human subjects research. *Erasmus Journal for Philosophy and Economics, 5*, 22–44. Retrieved from http://ejpe.org/pdf/5-1-art-2.pdf

British Academy. (2012). *A position statement – Society counts, quantitative skills of social sciences and humanities.* London: Author.

British Academy. (2014). *High level strategy group for quantitative skills.* Author [Website]. Retrieved from http://www.britac.ac.uk/policy/High_Level_Strategy_Group_for_QS.cfm

Buckley, J., Brown, M., Thomson, S., Olsen, W., & Carter, J. (2015). Embedding quantitative skills into the social science curriculum: Case studies from Manchester. *International Journal of Social Research Methodology, 18*(5), 495–510.

Centre for Multilevel Modelling. (2014). *Learning environment for multilevel methodology and applications.* Retrieved from http://www.bristol.ac.uk/cmm/learning/online-course/

Corti, L., Van den Eynden, V., Bishop, L., & Woollard, M. (2014). *Managing and sharing research data: A guide to good practice.* London: Sage. ISBN 978-1-44626-726-4.

Corti, L., & Watkins, W. (2004, Summer/Fall 4-5). Guest editors' notes. In L. Corti & W. Watkins (Eds.), *IASSIST quarterly* [Special edition on statistical literacy]. Retrieved from http://www.iassistdata.org/downloads/iqvol282_3editor_0.pdf

Corti, L., Witzel, A., & Bishop, L. (Eds.). (2005, special issue). Secondary analysis of qualitative data. *Forum Qualitative Sozialforschung/Forum: Qualitative Social Research, 6*. Retrieved from http:www.qualitative-research.net/index.php/fqs/article/view/498

Crow, G., & Edwards, R. (Eds.). (2012, special issue). Perspectives on working with archived textual and visual material in social research. *International Journal of Social Research Methodology, 15*. doi:10.1080/13645579.2012.688308

Digital Preservation Coalition. (2014). *Digital preservation training programme.* Author [Website]. Retrieved from http://www.dpconline.org/training/digital-preservation-training-programme

DCC. (2013). *Digital curation training for all.* Author [Website]. Retrieved from http://www.dcc.ac.uk/training

EPSRC. (2011). *EPSRC policy framework on research data.* Author [Website]. Retrieved from http://epsrc.ac.uk/about/standards/researchdata

ESRC. (2012). *Secondary data analysis initiative.* Author [Website]. Retrieved from http://www.esrc.ac.uk/research/skills-training-development/sdai/

ESRC. (2013). *Big data network.* Author [Website]. Retrieved from http://www.esrc.ac.uk/research/major-investments/Big-Data/

ESRC, BSA and HAPS. (2010). *International benchmarking review of UK sociology.* Swindon: ESRC.

Green, A., & Gutman, M. (2006). Building partnerships among social science researchers, institution-based repositories and domain specific data archives. *OCLC Systems and Services: International Digital Library Perspectives, 23*, 35–53. Retrieved from http://deepblue.lib.umich.edu/handle/2027.42/41214

Hamilton, P., Gossman, P., & Southern, K. (2014). *Developing innovative support structures for students undertaking small-scale research projects in work settings.* The Higher

Education Authority [Website]. Retrieved from https://www.heacademy.ac.uk/sites/default/files/resources/Glyndwr_final.pdf

Haynes, J., & Jones, D. (2012). A tale of two analyses: The use of archived qualitative data. *Sociological Research Online, 17*(2), 1. Retrieved from http://www.socresonline.org.uk/17/2/1.html

Inter-University Consortium for Political and Social Research. (2009). *Age and attitudes about the rights of homosexuals: A data-driven learning guide*. Author, University of Michigan [Website]. Retrieved from http://dx.doi.org/10.3886/gayrights

Kelly, A. (2012). *Introducing sociology students to quantitative research methods*. UK Data Service Case Study, University of Essex [Website]. Retrieved from http://ukdataservice.ac.uk/use-data/data-in-use/case-study/?id=19

Kilburn, D., Nind, M., & Wiles, R. (2014a). Learning as researchers and teachers: The development of a pedagogical culture for social science research methods? *British Journal of Educational Studies, 62*, 191–207. doi:10.1080/00071005.2014.918576

Kilburn, D., Nind, M., & Wiles, R. (2014b). *Short courses in advanced research methods: Challenges and opportunities for teaching and learning*. Southampton: National Centre for Research Methods Report, NCRM, University of Southampton. Retrieved from http://eprints.ncrm.ac.uk/3601/2/advanced_methods_short_courses.pdf

Kirton, A., Campbell, P., & Hardwick, L. (2014). *Developing applied research skills through collaboration in extra-academic contexts*. The Higher Education Authority [Website]. Retrieved from https://www.heacademy.ac.uk/sites/default/files/resources/Liverpool.pdf

Kottmann, A. (2011). Reform of doctoral training in Europe: A silent revolution? In J. Enders, H. de Boer, & D. Westerheijden (Eds.), *Reform of higher education in Europe* (pp. 29–43). Rotterdam: Sense.

Kynaston, D. (2005, January). The uses of sociology for real-time history. *Forum: Qualitative Social Research, 6*(1). Retrieved from http://www.qualitative-research.net/index.php/fqs/article/view/503

Leston-Bandera, C. (2013). Ten tips to develop engaging undergraduate research methods teaching. Blog post. *Political Insight*. Political Studies Association [Website]. Retrieved from http://www.psa.ac.uk/political-insight/blog/ten-tips-develop-engaging-undergraduate-research-methods-teaching

Library of Congress. (2013). *Digital preservation outreach and education*. Library of Congress [Website]. Retrieved from http://www.digitalpreservation.gov/education/curriculum.html

MacInnes, J. (2012). Quantitative methods teaching in UK higher education: The state of the field and how it might be improved. *HEA Social Sciences teaching and learning summit: Teaching research methods*. Retrieved from http://www-new1.heacademy.ac.uk/assets/documents/Events/SS_assets/Blog/MacInnes_fullpaper1.pdf

National Centre for Research Methods. (2014). *Current research programme*. University of Southampton [Website]. Retrieved from http://www.ncrm.ac.uk/research/

Nuffield Foundation. (2012). *Programme backgrounds – Promoting a step change in the quantitative skills of social science undergraduates*. London: Nuffield Foundation..

Nuffield Foundation. (2013). *Why Q-step? Hopes for wider change*. Presentation. Author. Retrieved from https://www.heacademy.ac.uk/sites/default/files/resources/4_4_Nuffield_panel.pdf

Research Councils UK. (2011). *Common principles on data policy*. Author. Retrieved from http://www.rcuk.ac.uk/research/datapolicy/

Research Councils UK. (2012). *Research councils UK policy on open access*. Author. Retrieved from http://www.rcuk.ac.uk/research/openaccess/policy/

Royal Statistical Society. (2014). *Getstats – Statistical literacy for all*. Author. Retrieved from http://www.getstats.org.uk

SCONUL. (2014). *Shared and collaborative services strategy group*. Author [Website]. Retrieved from http://www.sconul.ac.uk/page/shared-and-collaborative-services-strategy-group

Silver, C., & Woolf, N. (2015). From guided-instruction to facilitation of learning: The development of five-level QDA as a CAQDAS pedagogy that explicates the practices of expert users. *International Journal of Social Research Methodology, 18*, 527–543.

Sloan, L. (2013). *Innovation in the assessment of social science research methods, social sciences blog*. The Higher Education Academy. Retrieved from http://blogs.heacademy.

ac.uk/social-sciences/2013/11/11/innovation-in-the-assessment-of-social-science-research-methods/

Smith, E. (2008). *Using secondary data in educational and social research*. Oxford: OUP Press.

Strayhorn, T. (2009). The (in)effectiveness of various approaches to teaching research methods. In M. Garner, C. Wagner, & B. Kawulich (Eds.), *Teaching research methods in the social sciences* (pp. 119–130). Farnham: Ashgate Publishing Group.

Trzesniewski, K., Donnellamn, B., & Lucas, R. (Eds.). (2011). *Secondary data analysis: An introduction for psychologists*. Washington, DC: APA.

Turton, J. (2012). *Getting sociology students into archived qualitative data*. UK Data Service Case Study, University of Essex. Retrieved from http://ukdataservice.ac.uk/use-data/data-in-use/case-study/?id=107

UK Data Service. (2014a). *Case studies of re-use*. Author [Website]. Retrieved from http://ukdataservice.ac.uk/use-data/data-in-use.aspx

UK Data Service. (2014b). *Prepare and manage data*. Author [Website]. Retrieved from http://ukdataservice.ac.uk/manage-data

UK Data Service. (2014c). *Events at the UK Data Service*. Author [Website]. Retrieved from http://ukdataservice.ac.uk/news-and-events/events.aspx

University of Bristol. (2014). *Data.bris*. Author [Website]. Retrieved from http://data.bris.ac.uk/research/

University of Edinburgh. (2014). *Research data management guidance*. Author [Website]. Retrieved from http://www.ed.ac.uk/schools-departments/information-services/research-support/data-library/research-data-mgmt

University of Michigan. (2014). *Social network analysis course*. Coursera [Website]. Retrieved from https://www.coursera.org/course/sna

University of Southampton. (2014). *Web science: How the web is changing the world course*. Author, FutureLearn [Website]. Retrieved from https://www.futurelearn.com/courses/web-science-2014-q3

Urban Big Data Centre. (2014). *Overview*. Author [Website]. Retrieved from http://ubdc.ac.uk/

Vartanian, T. (2010). *Secondary data analysis*. New York, NY: OUP.

Vitae. (2013). *Transforming professional development for researchers: Vitae achievements and impact 2008–2012*. Author [Website]. Retrieved from https://www.vitae.ac.uk/vitae-publications/reports/report-achievements-vitae-2008-2012.pdf

Williams, M., Payne, G., Hodgkinson, L., & Poole, D. (2008). Does British sociology count? Sociology students' attitudes toward quantitative methods. *Sociology, 42*, 1003–1021.

Using video and dialogue to generate pedagogic knowledge: teachers, learners and researchers reflecting together on the pedagogy of social research methods

Melanie Nind, Daniel Kilburn and Rose Wiles

National Centre for Research Methods, University of Southampton, Highfield, Southampton, UK

> Developments in pedagogical knowledge in the teaching of social research methods have largely been generated through teachers reflecting on their practice. This paper presents an alternative approach to generating data through reflective dialogue between researchers, teachers and learners. The approach incorporates elements of video stimulated recall and reflective dialogue within focus group interviewing. The rationale and affordances are discussed in relation to the goals of discussing teachers' pedagogical decision-making and learners' experience of, and response to, various pedagogical practices. The context is a study of capacity-building short courses in advanced social science research methods, specifically courses on: multi-modal analysis, computer-assisted qualitative data analysis software, multi-level modelling, and systematic review. The paper examines the methodological challenges of capturing the everyday realities of methods classrooms for teachers and learners and the affordances of using dialogue on observed teaching sessions to gain further insight into each other's thinking and action. It concludes with lessons learned about methodological and pedagogical processes and an argument about the value of bringing methods and standpoints together in creative dialogue.

Introduction

A need has been identified in the UK (HaPS, 2010; Lynch et al., 2007; McVie, Coxon, Hawkins, Palmer, & Rice, 2008), Europe (Kottmann, 2011) and beyond, to build capacity in both the development of advanced research methods in the social sciences and their application to challenging research problems. Building that capacity requires investment of resources and considerable attention has been paid to the organizational elements (Moley & Seale, 2010; Payne & Williams, 2011). Building capacity also demands attention to the ways in which methods are taught and learned and to enhancing pedagogical knowledge among those involved. The research literature on the pedagogy of advanced research methods is relatively limited indicating that more research is needed to stimulate a pedagocial culture (Earley, 2014; Kilburn, Nind, & Wiles, 2014; Wagner, Garner, & Kawulich, 2011).

This is an Open Access article distributed under the terms of the Creative Commons Attribution License (http://creativecommons.org/licenses/by/4.0/), which permits unrestricted use, distribution, and reproduction in any medium, provided the original work is properly cited.

The research discussed in the paper started from a premise that better understanding of the pedagogical demands of teaching research methods is needed, particularly in relation to short courses in advanced or innovative methods that are key to the UK Economic and Social Research Council strategy. This includes understanding the particular pedagogical practices and pedagogical content knowledge (PCK) (Shulman, 1986) associated with advanced social science research methods – how those with advanced methodological competence translate their knowledge of methods into a form that others can comprehend and use. Our research questions included:

(1) What distinctive pedagogical challenges arise in teaching advanced, or innovative, social science research methods?
(2) How do teachers and learners respond to those challenges?
(3) What is the nature of teachers' PCK and learners' insight into this?

We aimed to address these questions by engaging teachers and learners in pursuing pedagogical understanding with us. In taking their knowledge seriously we were treading a balance between not wishing to 'distort, destroy or reconstruct' (Fenstermacher, 1994, p. 11) that knowledge and wishing to inform rather than merely illuminate knowledge and practice. Thus, rather than just treading softly, we were directly engaged in the methodological challenges about how to involve, rather than pass judgement on, research methods teachers and learners. Consequently, the research had elements of partnering in dialogue for knowledge creation.

The first, *expert panel* component, adapted from the work of Galliers and Haung (2012), was concerned with gaining broader or more conceptual insights into knowledge, views and experiences related to methods teaching and learning. The second, *close up* component was concerned with specific knowledge generated in relation to particular teaching and learning events. This involved using video stimulated focus group discussion with teachers and learners immediately following observed and recorded methods training and is the focus of this paper.

The challenge

Shulman (1986) drew attention to how content is taught as a missing component of education research, and particularly to questions of how teachers formulate explanations, decide on content and how to represent it, ask students about it and respond to misunderstanding. Shulman acknowledges teachers' expertise in the content they teach as a starting point for their teaching, but urges pedagogical research to focus on how this expertise is used in terms of process and becomes transformed into a form that is comprehensible to learners. Thus, alongside other knowledge (of content, curricula, learners, educational 'ends'), he proposes that teachers hold a mix of general pedagogical knowledge ('those broad principles and strategies of classroom management and organization that appear to transcend subject matter' [Shulman, 1987, p. 8]) and PCK which is pedagogical knowledge specific to the subject matter. PCK has become an established concept in teacher education, enhanced within extended models (see Kind, 2009). Only occasionally has it been questioned in terms of being too static (Banks, Leach, & Moon, 2005) or regarding whether content and pedagogy are more inherently imbued with each other than the concept implies, in that 'knowledge is … always already pedagogical' (Segall, 2004,

p. 291). In the arena of teaching advanced social research methods, teachers' subject matter knowledge comes from their familiarity with the methods in the context of applying them and from their own advanced methodological literacy. This may inherently shape their pedagogical practices but their PCK is under-explored and indeed challenging to explore.

PCK 'embodies the aspects of content most germane to its teachability' (Shulman, 1986, p. 9). This knowledge of how to powerfully represent ideas, which analogies and examples are effective, what makes grasp of specific topics easy or difficult and so on translates into active knowing (see Kind, 2009), skills and practices. This is the 'craft knowledge', the practical wisdom that interacts with rather than sits in opposition to theoretical knowledge, the study of which cannot lead to prescriptions for teaching but 'should attempt to surpass the idiosyncratic level of individual narratives' (van Driel, Verloop, & de Vos, 1998, p. 674). Such knowledge is tacit, practical and situated (Traianou, 2006); it is often not visible through observing teaching, nor easily drawn to mind through interviewing teachers about their teaching in the abstract. The development of PCK involves complex interaction of dynamic forces which, Özmanter (2011) argues, teachers need to reflect on if they are to beneficially transform their pedagogical practices. Thus, we aimed to glean insights into PCK and pedagogical practices in teaching social research methods through a combination of observing and interviewing involving video stimulated recall and reflection.

Video stimulated recall is an established method for helping teachers to reflect on their practice (see Moyles, Adams, & Musgrove, 2002; Pirie, 1996; Powell, 2005). Debate about refining the method focuses on the timing of the stimulated recall; Lyle (2003) argues from experience that for accurate recall it is important to conduct the video-stimulated interview as soon after the event as possible, though tiredness can work against this. While one can never quite get to what teachers (and learners) were thinking at the time (as this is not always knowable to the people themselves), the goal of getting as close as possible requires overcoming challenges of scheduling. Using video rather than still images brings further technical challenges and Dodd (2014) notes the difficulties within practitioner research of leaving a camera to capture the activity of the busy classroom and facilitating adequate playback.

Video has been used with teachers to stimulate not just recall but also reflective dialogue. Moyles, Hargreaves, Merry, Paterson, and Estarte-Sarries (2003) used this approach extensively when researching interactive teaching in primary schools, whereby joint viewing of their work provided the participating teachers with 'an opportunity to reflect with a knowledgeable research partner on one's own teaching' (p. 4). Their joint reflection was replicated by Challen (2013), again with primary school teachers, and with the intention of valuing and triangulating different perspectives and data sources. The approach has the potential to inform practice as well as research (see e.g. Clarke, 1997; Powell, 2005). There are benefits for participating teachers reflecting on their own work, but also valuable and often missed (Alexander, 2000) potential insights to be contributed by learners, and alternative, perceptive and, as Krull, Oras, and Sisask (2007) found, critical insights that can be contributed by uninvolved teachers.

The use of video to stimulate recall, reflection and dialogue is very different from its use for primary analysis. In analysing the talk that is stimulated, the focus is more on the thinking behind the action (including the elusive PCK) and the responses to it, than on the action itself. In turn, these are intertwined as knowledge in action for, as Shulman (1987) argues, pedagogical practices both reflect and stimulate thoughtfulness. Thus, in this research we followed the guidance of Alexander (2000, p. 269) to 'talk with whom we watch'. While recall is aided by immediate follow-up questioning based on the video (Morgan, 2007), reflection is aided by time spent with the video to consider it alongside reflective prompts. One way to do this is for participants to view the video in their own time, selecting episodes for discussion and gaining a sense of ownership as well as authentic dialogue (Challen, 2013). Careful preparation of pre-selected video clips can lead to more focused data generation but it may be necessary for episodes to be hastily selected by researchers from field notes or spontaneously sought in the moment of the discussion. One way of making up for lack of reflection time is using careful questioning and prompting (Challen, 2013; Moyles et al., 2003) but this may feel less comfortable as partnership research. Fenstermacher (1994, p. 4) discusses 'the difference between knowledge generated by university-based researchers and that generated by practicing teachers'; we were interested in knowledge generated by both of these, plus learners, in dialogue. We wanted teachers and learners involved in this research to be co-producers of knowledge, working with primary data and analytic units that they could connect with.

The research

Our emphasis in the close up component of the study was on facilitating a small number of video stimulated focus group discussions and exploring how to optimise the usefulness of these for fruitful data generation in relation to the three stated research questions, particularly the third about the nature of teachers' PCK and learners' insight into this. The starting point was the selection of teaching/training events and the sampling strategy for the participants. Selection was based on the need for the courses: to be short (1–4 days); to represent advanced or innovative social research methods training[1] (our overall remit); and to be taught by people with sufficient confidence in their practice and interest in the project to be comfortable with participation (as part of our ethics protocol) so as not to cause undue stress and to facilitate benefits from participation. An additional practical concern was that the course schedule needed to allow for a focus group to be added to the end of the day (thus excluding some potentially interesting yet longer one-day courses) as convening the group at a later date would be impractical. Together the courses needed to cover a variety of research methods (even if, as it transpired, they focused on their more technical aspects). Four short course events were chosen from the sampling frame of those advertised on the training database of the National Centre for Research Methods, one each on multi-modality (MM), computer-assisted qualitative data analysis software (CAQDAS), multi-level modelling (MLM) and systematic review (SR).

We engaged in extensive preparation with the technical challenges intertwined with the methodological and ethical decision-making. A core aim was for teachers and learners to enter into dialogue in reflecting back on a specific teaching/training event. Hence, we had rejected the option of separate focus groups for teachers and learners – a scenario in which the benefit of more candid comment would be outweighed by the sense that the learners, teachers and researchers were passing judgement on one another. The desire for them to come together in dialogue over the pedagogical processes at work also guided the need for two camera angles, one focused on the teacher(s) and one on the learners. During video playback, the aim was to simultaneously show these different perspectives by combining the camera angles into a single video.

To achieve immediate playback a novel technical solution was required involving the use of a high-powered laptop to synchronously capture video from two separate cameras together with a boundary-style microphone suited to recording group discussion. Where footage from multiple cameras would normally need to be combined, along with audio recordings, during *post hoc* video editing, this approach allowed us to capture and combine the different camera angles and audio as a 'live' recording that could be available for immediate playback. Having trialled various equipment we selected two high definition wide-angled cameras with the facility to output (or 'stream') video in a format that could be captured by a laptop computer. These cameras also had the advantage of being very compact and lightweight, allowing them to be mounted inconspicuously in convenient areas of the teaching rooms (typically on suction-cup mounts) thus hopefully minimising stress on teachers and learners. One camera was angled towards the front of the room to capture the teacher(s); the other was angled towards the learners to provide a perspective similar to that of the teacher. The boundary microphone was positioned towards the middle of the room to capture audio from both the teacher and the learners. Software was used to combine the video and audio sources into a single recording, using either 'picture-in-picture' or 'split-screen' formats. For a more detailed discussion of the technical options explored for this project, see Kilburn (2014).

Access to each course was negotiated with the teacher/trainer first. Upon recruiting the teachers we contacted the enroled learners to explain the research, their right to opt out from being video recorded, and their option to participate in the focus group. No learners opted not to be video recorded and between around a quarter and three-quarters opted into the focus group. For each course we opted to observe one whole training day in real time (two of the courses were 1-day events, one 3-day and one 4-day) while making the video recording. This involved one researcher monitoring the video capture and adjusting the equipment as necessary, one making a detailed qualitative observational record, and one focused on recording the timing of procedural events and critical moments to aid their identification for playback (this being particularly important as a day's-worth of video footage was typically captured).

At the start of each event we reminded learners of the aims and procedures in the research. In terms of ethics, we wanted to create a research environment that did not induce undue stress. The information for participants emphasised that this was a collaborative and not judgemental exploratory probing of pedagogical practices. During the sessions we sat at the back or side, making ourselves unobtrusive without disguising the purpose of our presence. At breaks in the teaching the three of us conferred about key moments that might be useful for the focus group discussion – those that marked a critical point in the session or that illustrated what we felt was an interesting pedagogical event or strategy. At the end of the teaching and before the focus group began, we arranged an informal circle of seating, provided refreshments, gathered informed consent forms, provided £10 retail vouchers as a thank you for participation and answered any questions. This helped to establish a relaxed ambience.

The focus group discussions lasted for approximately fifty minutes and involved one to three teachers and between three and thirteen learners. The discussions were audio recorded and transcribed. The topic guide was planned to include a warm-up question steered to the teachers about the challenges they perceived in teaching the particular material/skills, with prompts about what guided the approach and whether anything new was tried. The learners were then invited to discuss what was challenging to learn. The topic guide moved to presentation of video clips for discussion and then to inviting the teacher and then learners to identify particular parts of the session that they would like to review in the video and reflect on. Prompts were about the reasons for the selection, what was challenging at that time and how they felt. The planned ending was an open invitation to add topics for attention in the study. Focus group discussions differed in how free-flowing they were and in the amount of video incorporated and how it was used. Focus group transcripts were each thematically analysed by two researchers using (and adding to) themes agreed by the research team in response to the initial thematic analysis of the expert panel component. NVivo and freehand coding were used in a complementary fashion. Features of grounded theorising and constant comparison were used to identify and develop themes iteratively from the ongoing data-collection and analysis. Emergent themes were discussed among the research team leading to refinement of the coding scheme. The central themes emerging from the data broadly concerned the individual approaches taken by the learners and teachers, the way in which teaching was conducted and experienced, and the broader context in which these training sessions took place. The product of this process, which was shaped by the interests of both teachers and learners, was shared with the teachers when formulating this paper; approaching the learners again at this point was not feasible.

Reflection: the challenges, successes and findings
Challenges

In the event, the role played by the video in stimulating recall and reflection was smaller than anticipated. This was in part a matter of redundancy: as the focus groups immediately followed the courses participants seemed keen and competent to reflect on the session without the need for audio-visual stimuli. It was, therefore, sometimes judged – in the moment – to be fruitless rather than fruitful to interrupt the flow of dialogue to incorporate the video. Sometimes the learners made this judgement for themselves, such as in the focus group following training in SR when the learners were offered the opportunity to select video and instead opted to discuss active learning time in the training without recourse to the video for recall. Despite our real-time observation of the sessions, note-taking, discussion during breaks, and advanced technology, it also proved challenging to identify provocative video clips from the days' training in the brief preparation time available between the session and the focus group. It was harder still to triangulate the notes and time codes to identify precise episodes mentioned in dialogue. Typically, we therefore limited the use of the video to two or three clips, lasting no more than a couple of minutes. Given more time for reflection between training event and focus group it is likely that we would have made more use of the video.

The role of the video was also diminished by the sense in which the real life experience did not always adequately translate into the video format. There were many occasions when we were enthused about the pedagogical significance of something that had happened in the session, having independently recorded it as a critical moment in our notes, but often when we showed a video clip of this to the group there was a muted response. Even we (sometimes somewhat embarrassingly after an enthusiastic build-up to the clip) could not see on video what we felt in real time observation. While the discussion that followed the playback on such occasions was illuminating, it was not animated. One reading of this is that the quality of the video and/or sound sometimes failed to adequately capture what was taking place during the training itself. This presented a considerable methodological hurdle as the quality of the recording/playback was affected by factors beyond our control. In some cases, low lighting or high levels of ambient noise impacted on the audio-visual quality of our recordings and in others the recording was of a high quality but the venue's playback equipment was not. We also felt that, by the time everyone viewed the video together they were tired and less liable to be moved (though the evidence for this is hard to establish). Being relatively uninterested in the moment-by-moment pedagogical unfolding of the session could explain the low impact of the video clips for the learners, possibly even the teachers, although this was not the impression that we gained from the respondents themselves. It may just be that the ephemeral is just that; video can record and translate experience but it cannot replace or recreate experience. This is not to say that the role of video is negated, rather that expectations of it need to be adjusted.

The video seemed to be more effective, not when it was a trigger to recall and reflection, but when it was a response to it. In the discussion following the CAQDAS training, video was used naturally as a contribution to the discussion, not chosen by the learner but triggered by her reference to the teacher co-teaching with a course participant and the researcher finding a video clip of this. This led into a new discussion about the diagram the teacher used and her reflection on the newness of this for her. The discussion emerged from genuine shared focus, making sense of something that was significant for all. This may have been helped by the group being very small (three learners) which added informality to the task, for example:

Melanie:	… are there other sort of moments that we can discuss that were significant in any way?
Dom (learner):	Yeah, I have a moment.
Melanie:	You have a moment; share it with us!
Dom:	I would like to make it the other way, what's your guess what was my moment! [laughter] Anyway, I'll tell you!

These particular learners were also people who supported others in learning research methods and so their level of interest in the pedagogic dimension was high. They were unusual as participants in identifying video clips and drawing out their importance as seen in this excerpt:

Melanie:	So that's a deliberate.
Nadia (teacher):	That's a deliberate thing, yeah.
Kim (learner):	That worked really well.
Melanie:	Learning by our mistakes.
Daniel:	I can't remember where that is.
Natalie (learner):	That's quite near the end, yeah.
Video:	[1m0s]
Natalie:	None of us are responding. You [Nadia] went for a long time before we responded. Did you notice? You talked for a long time about that before, and it was Dom who finally responded, the rest of us

	just sat there. And then we turned when Dom said it. You turned last I think Kim.
Kim:	Yeah, I think.
Natalie:	[to Nadia] You were feeling conscious about you wanted a reaction because you kept going and you moved around and you kind of sat down and you [.]
Nadia:	I think I was, and I don't know what I was thinking.
Melanie:	And was that the time when you said 'shall I say it again?', that was a good moment?
Kim:	Yeah, so that was when I didn't understand something, actually, 'shall I say it again?'

In contrast it is clear from the transcript of the focus group of advanced quantitative learners that sometimes the observed episode resonated with us as researchers only; we had the whole research picture and others did not. Hence, when we showed a video clip of the teacher drawing on her own experience and learning from her errors we could articulate why it mattered to us:

Melanie:	So other researchers, trainee researchers or whatever, early career researchers, have said to us that it matters that the people teaching them have real-life experience of using that model. Does that resonate with you [learners] or does it matter that Abigail's [teacher] used that?
Daniel:	And encountered, not a problem, but an area of confusion or uncertainty in these things, so actually you know, that their method wasn't perfect.

The learners went on to echo some of the things that our interviewed experts had discussed, for example:

> ... when we are facing the same, similar kind of a problem we don't feel that we are alone or, so we feel a little bit more confident. So this kind of personal narratives or personal experiences sometimes are valuable as some kind of, give some kind of comfort that no, this is the first time my model has failed ... (Bruno)

Aside from as a possible aid in recalling the moment in question, the video had little direct impact in triggering this response.

The impact of the video may have been lessened because the atmosphere and context were missing in the playback. An event was funny, or informative, or critical as it played out because of where it was in the day, how everyone was feeling, or the interpersonal dynamic at that time. These factors were not replicable in the video. We had carefully chosen our equipment, camera angles and episodes, but we were not film makers seeking or able to intensify the moment. When we use anecdote – in teaching, interviewing or reporting of research – we craft it so that it serves our purpose. With the video we had neither the skill nor time for this. This may be where, with greater time, we could combine anecdote and video with greater effect.

Successes

One occasion when the video did bring a significant moment alive was instigated by Daniel and related to the teacher offering two subtly different graphs. The primary pedagogical tool was use of visuals, but the discussion turned first to the unplanned shared humour in the moment, helping to re-create it.

Melanie:	Yes, do you want to put those pictures up? There was the bit about the optician! The 'Is that better or worse?' moment!
Daniel:	Well I suppose the point ... we wondered about this, and whether it was by complement perhaps the different ways in which people learn this sort of material?
Video:	[0m50s]
Daniel:	So it felt like a key moment for us.
Melanie:	It was nice.
Anton (teacher):	It felt like one for me too.
Melanie:	It was nice, because it was the first moment of shared laughter in the group, so it was the first time, sitting at the back we went 'oh yeah they are all together sharing that moment'. Because it could be that you're in different worlds. Do you know what I mean? You can all be going through the same experience, but experiencing it very differently, but here you were all sharing that joke. But there aren't many kind of opportunities for laughs teaching this stuff are there, you know? [laughter]
Anton:	It's not that funny, no!
Melanie:	Is it me, or is it [the material] dry?!
Anton:	It's not that funny per se, and we do try, yeah. And I hadn't written that down in advance certainly.

The exposure of the positive role humour can play could perhaps enable this to become further developed as conscious pedagogical practice for this quantitative methods teacher.

Another example of powerful video use followed the training on SR in which the video seemed to be effective because of the strength of feeling of the learners:

Video:	[0m48s]
Daniel:	I think, well Melanie will probably say more about this than me, but I think we're interested in that in particular because it was one of the moments [when] you're quite engaged ...
Melanie:	There was nodding then, for the tape ... it wasn't very long ago [laughter] do you recall that moment?
Liz (learner):	Actually I disagreed very strongly with what was being said, but perhaps, I don't know if that came across that I did. Well I didn't say, I didn't say 'I strongly disagree'.

The learner moved on to explicate her ethical position and another learner defended the disciplinary perspective from her own position within it. The discussion, which was about how they were behaving in class related to their feelings and disciplinary backgrounds, was animated with much shared focus and laughter; Liz spoke of being glad to have had the chance to follow up the conversation in class and to explore the other learners' different positionality. This is turn led to the teachers seeking learner feedback on their strategy of not splitting the course down quantitative/qualitative or disciplinary lines. The role of the video itself in all this is unclear, but the facilitation of shared dialogue was crucial. In introducing the video Daniel stated our desire not to pre-empt too much, yet it was hard to resist flagging up what moved us. Nonetheless the video led to discussion about the things the learners said they would remember from the training.

With regard to process, the focus groups were successful in establishing a three-way dialogue and a feeling of the challenge of teaching and learning research methods being something we were all in together. Anton encouraged learners to select video clips: 'I'd be interested if you guys could pick key moments'. Nadia commented to the learners, 'I've got to work out what all your needs are' and later 'I feel like I haven't got enough, I have never got enough time to say what I want to say and to cover ... ' Learners joined in with the pedagogical contemplation: 'I think that was a hard session to teach ...' (SR) and teachers seized on the opportunity for useable feedback, e.g. 'what are better ways of getting people more involved?' (Abigail, MLM). They communicated strongly the usefulness of discussing the pedagogy with the learners, with one teacher (SR) sharing his anxieties about lack of control over the student-centred parts of the course; he responded to learners' arguments about the value of these parts, 'You're right, it's about holding my nerve'. The shared aspect was aided by teachers sometimes connecting with the learners by referring to their own experiences of learning the method (MM), thus creating a sense of common experience.

While the collaborative, dialogic approach was appreciated, the strangeness of the situation was also noted, such as with jokes about dressing for the camera (Anton). In one focus group (following a day on MM) the teacher commented:

Anne:	Weird isn't it?
Melanie:	Pulling apart a session after it's just happened?
Anne:	[to learners] I feel weird; you must feel weird.

In another (following MLM training) Anton responded: 'What was going on in my head is a very difficult, odd question to ask me'. As researchers we were sometimes compensating for weaknesses in video clarity and responding to the newness of the situation by providing probably too much explanatory narrative. Despite this strangeness, participants entered openly into dialogue. Anne (somewhat atypically among the teachers) nominated a video clip of genuine interest to her, because as she said this part of her pedagogic practice was new and: 'so I'm genuinely welcoming all your thoughts on that'. Seeing it again helped her to reflect:

> Yeah, I think I just quite like the fact it felt quite conversational, I felt quite relaxed at that point when I suppose there was some comments that were feeding on from other members; it wasn't like I was always asking the questions. It felt like it was really interesting, lots of interesting questions.

Despite a similar level of reflection other participants rarely drew on the video as a resource.

More findings

With regard to findings, the video stimulated dialogue contributed data within the (mix of a priori and emergent) themes already identified in the expert panel component: the individual approaches taken by the learners and teachers, the way in which teaching was conducted and experienced, and the broader context in which these training sessions took place. The close up component added detail to some of the more generic statements. For example, the issue of pacing within teaching emerged from the individual interviews as a challenge, and Nadia talked specifically about her approach of looking at learners' computer screens to monitor learner pace and thus inform her pace. The data also reinforced issues that had arisen, such as the challenge of poorly prepared learners; teachers explained that in teaching the intricacies of SR or CAQDAS it is not their job to teach research or analysis, but that essential knowledge of this kind sometimes needed to be imparted. The learners endorsed concern with the difficulty of advanced methods subject matter with comments like, 'it's the topic that's hard' and 'the terminology was hard' (CAQDAS). Interviewees in the first component had raised the question of starting points and in the close up component learners commented on appreciating preparatory material that allowed them to orient themselves ahead of the session (MM, MLM) or having the order of covering quantitative approaches ahead of qualitative approaches reversed (SR). Teachers commented on 'having to quickly ascertain where people are and quickly realise where I can start off at' (Nadia). The close up component also added nuanced layers to themes like diversity of expertise with Nadia reflecting on her concern to manage her potential vulnerability as a teacher when faced with a very experienced learner ('she's going to know more than I do') and learners, in turn, talking about how much they valued hearing from more or differently experienced peers (CAQDAS, SR).

We had invested in the video stimulated dialogue approach partly in the hope of teasing out PCK. In this we were rewarded by teachers making illuminative statements, such as:

> If I know I've got people in the room who have used another software, then that's a really good teaching mechanism for me, because when I'm saying something about one software and I compare it to how it works in the other software, that's often quite a good way of making something clear. (Nadia)

Moreover, their reflexivity was evident as they spoke of their pedagogical decision-making: 'there's an intention behind that' (Nadia) or 'that [combination of practical interwoven with input] was by design' (Sonya, SR). They referred to their learning through experience. For example Nadia noted her conscious strategy to address conceptual content before operational content, and that 'In the past, when I first started teaching, I was much more operational'; Simon (SR) even spoke of his decision, having tried a practical activity for teaching a specific aspect, never to do so again. In some cases the teachers were drawing on extensive explicit pedagogical thought, the SR teachers discussed how, in teaching teams, they came to handle the mix of quantitative, qualitative and mixed approaches to synthesis, including issues of sequencing and primacy. At other times the combination of video and question prompt was effective in drawing out what was otherwise invisible to them. Nadia's embodiment of her concepts, for example, was so visually powerful yet so unconsciously executed: 'I talk with my whole body don't I? I never realised that ... I had no idea that I moved my hands'. Moreover this tacit device was applauded by learner Natalie who fed back 'that's a very attractive quality ... it's a form of engagement ... it's that energy you exude'. Implicit PCK was teased out, enabling the teacher to explain. For example, after showing a short video clip following the MLM course a dialogue ensued in which the teacher seemed to be articulating unrehearsed thinking while drawing the learners in and making a teaching point to them.

Melanie:	We noted lots of times when you were doing the refreshing, the recapping, 'remember, remember', which I guess [relates] to what you were saying about – you have to keep with it otherwise if they say something like that, and you haven't remembered – how did you know whether they were with you?
Anton:	It's a good question. You don't know ... the tricky point I would say with those sorts of things is that you have to make an assumption,

you sense that people are still with you to a certain degree, otherwise we then have to put another slide in or another 5-min extended explanation as to why we did the same thing. And I think the reason I asked the question there was less about ensuring they had an answer and more about reminding people to think about the ideas from the day before, and some of that is that you know you just have to go back and look at things again another time, and I always remember from when I learn different things, that you don't pick up everything the first time, you really don't. But by trying to remind you that there's something there to think about, it's putting in those triggers that actually you've got to, you know this bit relates back to something that I did yesterday, so I can go back and have a look at that some other time.

This was one of many occasions when we were prompted to re-think what we had seen. Looking at the video in isolation would suggest a teacher moving on at pace, whose questions are rhetorical, perhaps just habit. But this dialogue presents an alternative explanation and potentially important PCK. It was also an occasion when having the learner response to the pedagogy being made transparent added more layers of detail to the emergent and co-constructed picture.

Melanie:	Although we had the cameras, we couldn't tell what you were writing down or thinking … What was going on in your heads?
Stuart (learner):	… you start to tell that you've remembered the thing that we did yesterday. Yeah, it makes you pay more attention and try to remember to think, because for example for this like centralising thing was not one of the things that I clearly understood, so I came like yeah, this is the thing, that's why we had this before, so like yeah, it underlined in my mind that centralising thing because yeah, maybe I may need to pay more attention …
Anton:	Did it make you feel more anxious that I asked you about it then?
Stuart:	Yeah.
Anton:	So I mean was it [a] bad thing?
Stuart:	No, no, not anxious, but like more of – they're of importance.
Anton:	Right.
Stuart:	Just like that, particular like thing, because you will see that it is related to something else or something further, so like it makes you feel like maybe I have to look back for this particular stuff.

Our researcher understanding of the teachers' different uses of questioning in their teaching could be checked, although again the result was a co-constructed understanding.

Melanie:	And I think you two were using questions quite differently. You [Anton] were often using them to flag up 'this is an important thing', whereas you [Abigail] were using them to check knowledge I think some of the time and to sometimes pull people in?
Abigail:	Yeah, to see if they've understood what I've explained, yes … one thing that I find really difficult with this sort of course generally is to get feedback from the course participants and see if they're still with you or not, and also I quite like to incorporate them, but it's quite difficult …

Prompted by a fresh video clip, the focus group reflected together on what was going on with the questioning in Abigail's approach. The videos stimulated the learners to make visible aspects of their practice, just as it did for the teachers' pedagogy. An excerpt of video clip shown in fast time without sound prompted recall as much as reflection, but also invited the learners back into a space they were occupying earlier in the day. Learner Joe reflected:

> I found myself personally trying to get through them [online exercises] as quick as I could, because I might have been a bit slower compared to other people, so I was conscious of having the hour to get it done. So, but then obviously I need to go back myself and revisit and take my time going through the material myself to get a good grasp of it, but yeah, no, they were very useful, those workshops I thought.

Equally importantly, the learners' involvement and willingness to be candid allowed for additional insight into their approaches to the training provided including identifying 'some areas where I feel almost too ignorant to ask can I have help' (Tara, SR).

Conclusion: A method fit for purpose?

The video stimulated focus group approach used in the close up component of this study demanded considerable resource including researcher time. This was warranted in that it provided a record of the key events and enabled various interpretations of them. While the ephemeral qualities of these moments were not always adequately captured by the video, the clips nevertheless offered useful stimulus material in the way Morgan, Fellows, and Guevara (2008) describe in helping the focus groups in navigating between these points in time. While in the MLM training the learners had seemed rather passive and expression-less, making it difficult to detect their engagement, in the focus group they asserted their full concentration. New perspectives emerged quite literally, as in the focus group following the CAQDAS training one of the learners referred to another as a disembodied voice as she had not seen his face from behind his computer screen. This was not see-able by us as researchers at the back, or by the teacher seated at the front, and so without the focus group dialogue would have been left unknown to us. This echoes Challen's (2013, p. 76) experience of the 'crucial role' played by video stimulated reflective dialogue in alerting her to 'discrepancies' between what she thought she had observed and the participants' explanations. More broadly, it illustrates the value of reflective dialogue involving teachers and learners as one means of enhancing the role of practitioner reflection as a basis for pedagogical insights into the teaching of research methods. Our common experience is that in place of individual, potentially flawed interpretations, this approach was able to produce imperfect but shared and more nuanced interpretations. We cannot know what we might have achieved in terms of reflective dialogue without the inclusion of video. The indications are that video is not always necessary but that it provides a shared focus, sometimes as a stimulus and sometimes as a reference point during the interaction.

Shulman (1987, p. 6) observed that 'teachers themselves have difficulty articulating what they know and how they know it'. Our approach enabled subtle aspects of the teachers' pedagogical decision-making that was invisible to us as researchers, probably unnoticed by learners and intangible to the teachers, become knowable. Using our methodological approach, even with the technical challenges and limitations discussed here, some of the tacit practical knowledge that Traianou (2006) argues is applied by teachers *in situ* became accessible to us as a small learning community of teachers, learners and researchers. We were responding to an opportunity to read the pedagogical environment critically (Segall, 2004).This does not create pedagogical knowledge in a form that is immediately useable by others. Nonetheless, in the methods capacity-building arena where there is limited work generating data about pedagogical thought in action the approach is valuable. We make no claim to video stimulated reflection and dialogue being the best way to generate evidence and ensure its use to inform the teaching of research methods. We do, however, maintain that there is more to gain from its application.

Acknowledgements
We gratefully acknowledge all the methodologists, teachers and learners who participated in this research.

Disclosure statement
No potential conflict of interest was reported by the authors.

Funding
This work was supported by Economic and Social Research Council National Centre for Research Methods [grant number RES-576-47-5001-01].

Note
1. Advanced training here is taken to mean at postgraduate level and beyond aimed at those who have already embarked on a research career, applying rather than merely knowing about methods, and even developing them.

References
Alexander, R. (2000). *Culture and pedagogy.* Oxford: Blackwell.
Banks, F., Leach, J., & Moon, B. (2005). Extract from new understandings of teachers' pedagogic knowledge'. *Curriculum Journal, 16*, 331–340. doi:10.1080/09585170500256446
Challen, D. (2013). *A pedagogical exploration of guided reading in three primary classrooms* (Doctoral dissertation, University of Southampton, United Kindom). Retrieved from http://eprints.soton.ac.uk/358500/

Clarke, D. (1997, November–December). *The emergence of meaning in classroom research*. Paper presented at the Conference of the Australian Association for Research in Education, Brisbane, Australia.

Dodd, M. (2014). *Making connections: Problems, progress and priorities – A practitioner's viewpoint* (Doctoral dissertation, University of Southampton, United Kindom). Retrieved from http://eprints.soton.ac.uk/366262/

Earley, M. (2014). A synthesis of the literature on research methods education. *Teaching in Higher Education, 19*, 242–253. doi:10.1080/13562517.2013.860105

Fenstermacher, G. D. (1994). Chapter 1: The knower and the known: The nature of knowledge in research on teaching. *Review of Research in Education, 20*, 3–56. doi:10.3102/0091732X020001003

Galliers, R. D., & Haung, J. C. (2012). The teaching of qualitative research methods in information systems: An explorative study utilizing learning theory. *European Journal of Information Systems, 21*, 119–134. doi:10.1057/ejis.2011.44

HaPS. (2010). *International benchmarking review of UK sociology*. HaPs (Heads and Professors of Sociology), ESRC & BSA.

Kilburn, D. (2014). *Methods for recording video in the classroom: Producing single and multi-camera videos for research into teaching and learning* (NCRM Working Paper). NCRM. Retrieved from http://eprints.ncrm.ac.uk/3599/

Kilburn, D., Nind, M., & Wiles, R. A. (2014). Learning as researchers and teachers: The development of a pedagogical culture for social science research methods? *British Journal of Educational Studies, 62*, 191–207. doi:10.1080/00071005.2014.918576

Kind, V. (2009). Pedagogical content knowledge in science education: Perspectives and potential for progress. *Studies in Science Education, 45*, 169–204. doi:10.1080/03057260903142285

Kottmann, A. (2011). Reform of doctoral training in Europe: A silent revolution? In J. Enders, H. de Boer, & D. Westerheijden (Eds.), *Reform of Higher Education in Europe* (pp. 29–43). Rotterdam: Sense Publishers.

Krull, E., Oras, K., & Sisask, S. (2007). Differences in teachers' comments on classroom events as indicators of their professional development. *Teaching and Teacher Education, 23*, 1038–1050.

Lyle, J. (2003). Stimulated recall: A report on its use in naturalistic research. *British Educational Research Journal, 29*, 861–878. doi:10.1080/0141192032000137349

Lynch, R., Maio, G., Moore, G., Moore, L., Orford, S., Robinson, A., … Whitfield, K. (2007). *ESRC/HEFCW scoping study into quantitative methods capacity building in Wales*. Cardiff: Cardiff University, ESRC and HEFCW.

McVie, S., Coxon, A., Hawkins, P., Palmer, J., & Rice, R. (2008). *ESRC/SFC scoping study into quantitative methods capacity building in Scotland*. University of Edinburgh, ESRC and SFC, Edinburgh.

Moley, S., & Seale, J. (2010). *A strategic framework for capacity building within the ESRC National Centre for Research Methods*. University of Southampton, National Centre for Research Methods, Southampton.

Morgan, A. (2007). Using video-stimulated recall to understand young children's perceptions of learning in classroom setting. *European Early Childhood Education Research Journal, 15*, 213–226. doi:10.1080/13502930701320933

Morgan, D., Fellows, C., & Guevara, H. (2008). Emergent approaches to focus groups research. In N. S. Hesse-Biber & P. Leavy (Eds.), *Handbook of emergent methods* (pp. 189–205). New York, NY: Guilford Press.

Moyles, J., Adams, S., & Musgrove, A. (2002). Using reflective dialogues as a tool for engaging with challenges of defining effective pedagogy. *Early Child Development and Care, 172*, 463–478. doi:10.1080/03004430214551

Moyles, J., Hargreaves, L., Merry, R., Paterson, F., & Estarte-Sarries, V. (2003). *Interactive teaching in the primary school: Digging deeper into meanings*. Maidenhead: Open University Press.

Özmanter, M. F. (2011). Rethinking about the pedagogy for pedagogical content knowledge in the context of mathematics teaching. *Eurasia Journal of Mathematics, Science & Technology Education, 7*, 15–27.

Payne, G., & Williams, M. (Eds.). (2011). *Teaching quantitative methods: Getting the basics right*. London: Sage.

Pirie, S. E. B. (1996, February). *Classroom video-recording: When, why and how does it offer a valuable source for qualitative research?* Paper presented at annual meeting of the North American Chapter of the International Group for the Psychology of Mathematics Education, Panama City.

Powell, E. (2005). Conceptualising and facilitating active learning: Teachers' video-stimulated reflective dialogues. *Reflective Practice, 6*, 407–418. doi:10.1080/14623940500220202

Segall, A. (2004). Revisiting pedagogical content knowledge: The pedagogy of content/the content of pedagogy. *Teaching and Teacher Education, 20*, 489–504.

Shulman, L. (1986). Those who understand: Knowledge growth in teaching. *Educational Researcher, 15*, 4–14. doi:10.3102/0013189X015002004

Shulman, L. (1987). Knowledge and teaching: Foundations of the new reform. *Harvard Educational Review, 57*(1), 1–23.

Traianou, A. (2006). Understanding teacher expertise in primary science: A sociocultural approach. *Research Papers in Education, 21*, 63–78. doi:10.1080/02671520500445466

van Driel, J. H., Verloop, N., & de Vos, W. (1998). Developing science teachers' pedagogical content knowledge. *Journal of Research in Science Teaching, 35*, 673–695. doi:10.1002/(SICI)1098-2736(199808)

Wagner, C., Garner, M., & Kawulich, B. (2011). The state of the art of teaching research methods in the social sciences: Towards a pedagogical culture. *Studies in Higher Education, 36*, 75–88. doi:10.1080/03075070903452594

Index

Note: Page numbers in **bold** type refer to figures
Page numbers in *italic* type refer to tables
Page numbers followed by 'n' refer to notes

abstract knowledge 74, 79
active learning 98
actors 102; human 65
Adriaensen, J.: *et al.* 43
advance organizers 80; expository 81
advanced training 120n
Advanced Training Initiative (ESRC) 2
Agamben, G. 62
Age and Attitudes about the Rights of Homosexuals Guide 98
agency: learners 76
Alexander, R. 110
analytic adeptness 76
analytic strategies 83, **83**
analytic tactics 83, **83**
analytic tasks 84
Analytical Planning Worksheets 73, 84–6, **85**
anti-empirical orientation 57
anti-quantitative attitudes 42
Application Programming Interfaces 95
Applied Quantitative Methods Network (Scotland) 2
appropriate pedagogies 73
ASDA 35
ATLAS.ti 80

barriers: to learning 31, **32**; structural 21–2
benefits of learning quantitative data 50, *52*
bias 12–14
big data 92–6
Blair, A. (Tony) **85**
blended learning: game-based 38n
Bloom, B.: *et al.* 43–4
Bloom's hierarchy 57
Brady, M.: and Howard, C. 4, 57–71
Brannen, J.: and O'Connell, R. 16
British Crime Survey (BCS) 44
British Election Study (BES) 53
British Journal of Sociology 26
British Social Attitudes (BSA) survey 45, 48, 55n

British social science 25–6
Brown, M.: *et al.* 3–5, 41–56
Browne, J. 34
Buckley, J.: *et al.* 3–5, 41–56
Budd, C.: *et al.* 27

camera angles 111, 114
Canada 3, 58, 69n
capacity-building 107, 120
CAQDAS (Computer Assisted Qualitative Data Analysis Software) 4, 107, 110, 113, 117–19; Networking Project (CNP) 74–6, 87, 88n
Carter, J.: *et al.* 3–5, 41–56
Challen, D. 109, 119
Chamberlain, M.J.: *et al.* 44
Chamberlain, S.: Payne, G. and Williams, M. 26
coding 112
cognitive domain 44
collaborative relationships 45, 49
Collins, K.T.: *et al.* 10
comfort zones 16, 22, 96, 100
competence: staff 25
competence/confidence building 25–40
component learners 117
computer software 5, 81
computer-assisted data analysis programs 17, 73, 83
confidence building 25–40
confident staff 35–7
confident students 36–7
contexts of refutation 64–5
Corti, L.: and Van den Eynden, V. 3–4, 91–105; and Watkins, W. 97
CPD system 35
Creswell, J.W.: *et al.* 10
critical theory 59, 63
culture: pedagogic 2–5, 9, 17, 20, 60, 107; shift 27
curriculum: development 49; substantive 42–4

123

INDEX

Curriculum Innovation and Researcher Development Initiatives (ESRC) 54

data: analysis 5, 19, 47, 67, 79–81, 86; empirical 48, 65–7; encryption 99–101; handling 94–5; qualitative 95, 99–101; sources *46*; storage 99, *see also* quantitative data
Data Archive (UK) 93, 100
data lifecycle: intervention points in 93, **93**
data management 3, 80
Data Service (UK) 48, 53, 95–7
data-set 45–7
De Broe, S.: *et al.* 42
Dearing, R. 34
decentralization 30
decision-making: pedagogical 117–19
Deleuze, G. 62
Departmental Strategic Plan (UK, 2013) 35
Derrida, J. 62
Digital Curation Centre (DCC) (UK) 97
digital data 93–5, 102
Digital Preservation Coalition (DPC) (UK) 97; training courses 97
disciplinary power 67
diversity 87, 117
Dodd, M. 109
Dunne, R.: *et al.* 27
Durrant, G.: *et al.* 42

Earley, M. 2, 9–10, 60
economic climate 91
Economic and Social Research Council (ESRC, UK) 2, 25–7, 38, 41–2, 54, 93, 108; Advanced Training Initiative 2; Curriculum Innovation and Researcher Development Initiatives 54; funded projects 26; National Centre for Research Methods (NCRM) 2–3, 94, 110; RDI/CI programmes 25, 29, 37; Research Development Initiative 92
effective pedagogies 73
Elaboration model 28
Ely, P.: and Ely, A. 34
empirical data 48, 65–7
empiricism 65–6
Englehart, M.: *et al.* 43–4
equality: gender 66
Estarte-Sarries, V.: *et al.* 109
Europe 97, 107
European Union (EU) 1
expository advance organizers 81

facilitation: instruction-led 75–6, 80–1; of learning 73–89
facilitation-led instruction 76–82
faculty training courses: mixed methods 20–1
faculty training mixed methods courses 20–1
Falkingham, J.: and McGowan, T. 44, 49, 54

Fellows, C.: Guevara, H. and Morgan, D. 119
feminism 66
feminist epistemologies 65
Fenstermacher, G.D. 110
Foucault, M. 59, 62, 67
freehand coding 112
Freire, P. 30
Frels, R.K.: *et al.* 10
Furst, E.: *et al.* 43–4

Galliers, R.D.: and Haung, J.C. 108
game-based blended learning 38n
Garner, M.: Kawulich, B. and Wagner, C. 2, 9, 60
gender equality 66
Goldring, J.E.: and Scott Jones, J. 3–5, 25–40
graduate training programs 9, 22
grounded theory 12, 80
Gubrium, J.F.: and Holstein, J.A. 66
Guevara, H.: Morgan, D. and Fellows, C. 119
guided instruction 73–89; pedagogy 80
Guskey, T.R. 34

Haraway, D. 62
Hargreaves, L.: *et al.* 109
Hart, M.: *et al.* 27
Haung, J.C.: and Galliers, R.D. 108
Health Survey (England) 44
HEFCE (Higher Education Funding Council for England) 27
hegemony 67
Hesse-Biber, S. 3–4, 9–23
heterogeneity 75, 87
Higher Education Academy (HEA, UK) 3, 34; Social Sciences learning and teaching summit (2012) 94
Higher Education (HE) 1–2, 10, 97; community 42
Higher Education Institutions (HEIs) 74
Hill, W.: *et al.* 43–4
Hillier, J.: *et al.* 44
Hodgen, J.: Pepper, D. and London, C. 42
Hodgkinson, L.: *et al.* 28, 42
Holstein, J.A.: and Gubrium, J.F. 66
Houston Area Survey (USA) 98
Howard, C.: and Brady, M. 4, 57–71
Howel, D.: *et al.* 17–18
human actors 65
human agency 59

ideology 13
immigration 45–6
incremental learning 30
inequality 52
information security practices: robust 91
institutionalism 62–4
instruction-led facilitation 75–6, 80–1
International Benchmarking Review of Sociology 26, 94

INDEX

international relations 62
Interuniversity Consortium for Political and Social Research's Data-Driven Learning Guides (USA) 98
intervention points in data lifecycle 93, **93**
interview society 66
ISDA 29–30, 34–5

Jensen, K.D.: *et al.* 10
Jisc 97

Kahoot quizzes 33, 38n
Kawulich, B.: Wagner, C. and Garner, M. 2, 9, 60
Kerremans, B.: *et al.* 43
Kilburn, D.: *et al.* 4, 10, 17, 60–1, 66, 92, 107–22
kinaesthetic learning 33
knowledge: abstract 74, 79; building 11–13, 77; mathematical 42; pedagogic 107–22; pedagogical 1–7, 108, 120; pre-existing 64; subaltern 67
Krathwohl, D.: *et al.* 43–4
Krull, E.: Oras, K. and Sisask, S. 109

Land, R.: and Meyer, J.H.F. 31
Law, J.: and Urry, J. 66
learners 3–5; agency 76; struggles 82–3
learning: active 98; barriers to 31, **32**
Learning Environment for Multilevel Modelling (LEMMA) 98
Leech, N.L.: *et al.* 10
Levine, A.: *et al.* 10–12, 20
Library of Congress (USA) 97; Digital Preservation Outreach and Education Programme 97
linguistics 94
London, C.: Hodgen, J. and Pepper, D. 42
Luttwak, E. 81–2
Lyle, J. 109

McGowan, T.: and Falkingham, J. 44, 49, 54
MacInnes, J. 26–8
Mackingtosh, J.: *et al.* 17–18
Managing Research Data programme (UK, 2009–13) 97
Manchester Metropolitan University (MMU) 27, 37
Manchester (UK) 41–56; Q-Step programme 53
marginalization 41–2
marginalized populations 12
marketization 25
mathematical knowledge 42
maths anxiety 32
MAXQDA version (11) **85**
Mayer, R.E. 81
mental constructs 61
mental schema 61

Merry, R.: *et al.* 109
metadata 94–5, 98
methodological awareness 76
methodological vocabulary 68
methods training 1–2
Meyer, J.H.F.: and Land, R. 31
microcosm 27–9
Microsoft: Excel 84; Word 83–4
military studies 81
mixed methods 3–4
Moffatt, S.: *et al.* 17–18
Morgan, D.: Fellows, C. and Guevara, H. 119
Moyles, J.: *et al.* 109
multi-level modelling (MLM) 107, 110, 119
multi-modal analysis 107
multi-modality (MM) 110
multidisciplinary team-based teaching 21

National Centre for Research Methods (NCRM) 2–3, 94, 110
natural sciences 59
Newcastle upon Tyne (UK) 18
Nicolau, B.: *et al.* 10–12, 20
Nind, M.: *et al.* 4, 10, 17, 60–1, 66, 92, 107–22
Nuffield Foundation (UK) 27
NVivo 112

O'Connell, R.: and Brannen, J. 16
official truth 67
Olsen, W.: *et al.* 3–5, 41–56
online interfaces 47
online resources 73
ontological politics 66
Onwuegbuzie, A.J.: *et al.* 10
Open Educational Resources (OERs) 54
Oras, K.: Sisask, S. and Krull, E. 109
Özmanter, M.F. 109

paradigmatic assumptions 14
partnerships: teaching 45, *46*, 51
Paterson, F.: *et al.* 109
Payne, G.: *et al.* 28, 42; Williams, M. and Chamberlain, S. 26
pedagogic development 87
pedagogic theory 5
pedagogical culture 2–5, 9, 17, 20, 60
pedagogical gap 10
pedagogical knowledge 1–7
pedagogical orthodoxy 66
pedagogical philosophy 62
pedagogy 2–4, 30–2, 37, 92, 102; appropriate 73; constructivist 4; data management 92–6; effective 73; guided-instruction 80; mixed methods 11–13; reflective 10
Pepper, D.: London, C. and Hodgen, J. 42
philosophy: pedagogical 62; post-structuralist 57
Pluye, P.: *et al.* 10–12, 20

INDEX

Poade, D.: *et al.* 28, 42
political behavior 64
political theory 62–5
Porkess, R.: *et al.* 25
positivism 11, 59
post-positivism 14–15
post-structuralism 65, 69
post-structuralist philosophies 57
postgraduate level 120n
Powell, J.: *et al.* 42
power: dynamic 30; relations 59, 65
pre-enlightenment 65
pre-existing knowledge 64
Professional Standards Framework (UK, 2011) 34
professional training in data management 96–7
proficiency: technological 76
public service 69
publicly-funded research data 91

Q-Step programme (2014) 2, 25–7, 37, 53; Manchester 53
QS World Rankings (2014) 69n
qualitative data 95, 99–101; analysis 84
qualitative methods 4–5, 100
qualitative research 83, 86
quantitative data 18, 41, 45, 54; benefits of learning 50, **52**; learning benefits 50, **52**; students attitudes 50–1, *51*
quantitative learners 114
quantitative methods (QM) 4–5, 41, 44, 48–50, 53–4, 59, 115
quantitative orthodoxy 67
quantitative training 41, 52

randomized controlled trial (RCT) 18–19
RDI/CI programmes (ESRC) 25, 29, 37
Realistic Mathematics Education (RME) 43, 54n
Recurring Hourglass design 73–80, 86
reflective learning 10
reflective pedagogy 10
reflexivity 13–20
refutation: contexts of 64–5
Reigeluth, C.M. 79
research capacity 1–2
Research Development Initiative (ESRC) 92

scepticism 58, 68
SCONUL 101
Scotland: Applied Quantitative Methods Network 2
Scott Jones, J.: and Goldring, J.E. 3–5, 25–40
self-identifying 36
Shapley, K.L.: *et al.* 10
Shulman, L. 108–10, 119
Signoretta, P.: *et al.* 44
Silver, C. 74–81; and Woolf, N.H. 4–5, 73–89

Sisask, S.: Krull, E. and Oras, K. 109
skills: data management 4, 97–9
Skype 86
Slootmaeckers, K.: *et al.* 43
social media 94–5; Skype 86; Twitter 95; YouTube 20
social methodology 64
social realities 66
social research training methods 110
social science 1, 25–6, 50–4, 57–9, 65–8, 92–102; British 25–6; curriculum 41–56
social survey data (UK) 48
social survey Understanding Society (UK) 47
social world 15–16
sociology 47–8, 59, 94
Socrative discussions 33, 38n
software 5, 81; features 83; packages 73, 80, 86; statistical 44; tactics 82–3, **83**
software-assisted analyses 82
SPSS 28–32, 37, 47, 67
staff: competence 25; confident 35–7; training courses 29
staff-learners 33–4
statistical software 44
structural barriers 21–2
students: attitudes to quantitative data 50–1, *51*; confident 35–6; mental constructions about methods 63–4
subaltern knowledge 67
subjective qualitative component 19
substantive curriculum 42–4
substantive theory 50
systematic review (SR) 110, 115–16

Talab, R. 20
Tashakkori, A.: *et al.* 10; and Teddlie, C. 20
teachers 3–5
teaching modes 73, 80
team-based solutions 22
team-based teaching: approach 9; multidisciplinary 21
technical conceptual pedagogic practical (TCP) 30–4, **31**
technological proficiency 76
Teddlie, C.: and Tashakkori, A. 20
theory training 13
theory-question-methods continuum 13
Theory-testing Critical Discourse Analysis **85**
Thomson, S.: *et al.* 3–5, 41–56
threshold concept 31–2
Traianou, A. 119
training: advanced 120n; faculty 20–1; gaps 9; graduate program 9, 22; methods 1–2; professional, in data management 96–7; quantitative 41, 52; staff 29; theory 13
training courses (DPC) 97
translation 83–4, **85**
Translation Worksheets 84, 88n

INDEX

transmission models 69
transparency: to open access of research data 91; to re-use research data 91
twentieth century 1
Twitter 95
two-day model workshop **77–9**, 79–80, 86, 99–100

United Kingdom (UK) 1–2, 10, 25–9, 42–4, 54n, 81, 94–7, 107; Applied Quantitative Methods Network (Scotland) 2; British Crime Survey (BCS) 44; British Election Study (BES) 53; British Social Attitudes (BSA) survey 45, 48, 55n; British social science 25–6; Data Archive 93, 100; Data Service 48, 53, 95–7; Departmental Strategic Plan (2013) 35; Digital Curation Centre (DCC) 97; Digital Preservation Coalition (DPC) 97; Economic and Social Research Council (ESRC) 2, 25–7, 38, 41–2, 54, 93, 108; Higher Education Academy (HEA) 3, 34; Jisc 97; Managing Research Data programme (2009-2013) 97; Manchester 41–56; Newcastle upon Tyne 18; Nuffield Foundation 27; Professional Standards Framework (2011) 34; social survey data 48; social survey Understanding Society 47; training courses (DPC) 97; University of Bristol 97; University of Edinburgh 97
United States of America (USA) 3, 9, 20, 42, 59, 80, 97–8; Houston Area Survey 98; Interuniversity Consortium for Political and Social Research's Data-Driven Learning Guides 98; Library of Congress 97; University of Iowa 80
University of Bristol (UK) 97
University of Edinburgh (UK) 97
University of Iowa (USA) 80
upskilling 27
Urry, J.: and Law, J. 66
Using Software in Qualitative Research (Lewins and Silver) 75

Van den Eynden, V.: and Corti, L. 3–4, 91–105
virtual learning environment (VLE) 32
visual learning 33
Vitae 96
Vorderman, C.: *et al.* 27
Vygotsky, L.S. 33, 43

Wagner, C.: Garner. M. and Kawulich, B. 2, 9, 60
Watkins, W.: and Corti, L. 97
Weedon, C. 66
Wenger, E. 44
White, M.: *et al.* 17–18
Wiles, R.: *et al.* 4, 10, 17, 42, 60–1, 66, 92, 107–22
Williams, M.: Chamberlain, S. and Payne, G. 26; *et al.* 28, 42
Woolf, N.H. 74, 80–2; and Silver, C. 4–5, 73–89

YouTube 20